GLENDA JACKSON

David Nathan

Spellmount Ltd
Tunbridge Wells, Kent

Hippocrene Books Inc
New York

First published in UK in 1984 by
SPELLMOUNT LTD
12 Dene Way, Speldhurst
Tunbridge Wells, Kent TN3 0NX

British Library Cataloguing in Publication Data
Nathan, David
GLenda Jackson.—(Film & theatre stars)
1. Jackson, Glenda   2. Actors—Great
Britain—Biography
I. Title   II. Series
792.028'0924   PN2598.J3

ISBN 0-946771-35-9

First published in USA in 1984 by
HIPPOCRENE BOOKS INC
171 Madison Avenue
New York, NY 10016

ISBN 0 88254 924 3

Commissioning editor: Sue Rolfe
Series editor: John Latimer Smith
Cover design: Peter Theodosiou
Cover photo: Glenda Jackson as Cleopatra, 1978
Title page: Glenda Jackson as Hedda, *Hedda Gabler*, 1975

Printed & bound in Great Britain
by Anchor/Brendon Ltd, Tiptree, Essex

Contents

Acknowledgements

It would have been very foolhardy to attempt even this short book without help from the subject herself. I have had the benefit of several long conversations with Glenda Jackson and where I use the form 'she says' she has said it. In most other cases where she is quoted I have attributed the words to those who reported them in the first place and I am grateful for the opportunity of being able to draw on the work of so many able and perceptive journalists for she has been much interviewed in her time. Where I have sensed inaccuracy I have omitted.

I am also grateful to Janet Suzman, Susannah York, Dr Anthony Clare, Peter Crouch, Robert Enders, George Segal and Hugh Whitemore for their invaluable insights; to Judith Cheston and Jacqui Cusack of the Royal Shakespeare Company's Press Office, to Mary White of the Shakespeare Centre, Stratford-on-Avon, to the staff of the British Film Institute Library and the BBC Sound Archive for their skilled help and to the Observer newspaper for kind permission to quote in full Penelope Gilliatt's review of Glenda's performance as Ophelia.

I have omitted a bibliography, for where I have found a book useful I have acknowledged its assistance and, more important, its publisher in the text.

DAVID NATHAN, November, 1983

List of Illustrations

Glenda Jackson, 1983. *Photo*: John Nathan.

Hard Times

'Why, look you now, how unworthy a thing you make of me! You would play upon me, you would seem to know my stops, you would pluck out the heart of my mystery, you would sound me from my lowest note to the top of my compass – and there is much music, excellent voice in this little organ, yet cannot you make it speak. 'Sblood, do you think I am easier to be played on than a pipe?'
HAMLET, 3.2.

Mysteries do not flourish on the North West coast of England where Glenda May Jackson was born and raised. A few miles south are the Welsh and a few miles west are the Irish and it is as if all mystery has fled from Birkenhead to the more hospitable Celtic Fringe. In Birkenhead itself mystery rarely surrounds and almost never inhabits people. Those who would affect mystery are being fanciful and that would never do. There is work instead, and if you put your back into it you get good results; if you are sloppy and slack you get bad results and are not thought much of. So there is simply no mystery about Glenda May Jackson. She does good work so she gets good results.

'What's mysterious about it?' she asks, the vowels short, impatient, exasperated. 'You are given a prescribed world. The boundaries are drawn for you in a sense so that you have a narrowed vision. You know where to look. Quite often you start by looking in the wrong place, but you come back and look in the right one. There's a sort of detective element in discovering what the character's really like. But it doesn't follow that there's any mystery in me.

'I hate the idea of acting being some kind of mystical process. It isn't. I mean you do as much as an individual can do; you clear the undergrowth, you get rid of the stuff that isn't useful, you discard the ideas that aren't right. You do

11

everything you can, both physically and mentally, to be ready for something else to happen. That's what the performance is: is something else going to happen?'

A long pause, then, grudgingly, 'I suppose there's a kind of mystery element in that, but I don't like the idea of it being entirely a process that is without any kind of guiding sense.'

The mystery, then, is in the performance, not the person. The person can be described and her attitudes explored and examined. The undergrowth can be cleared and you get rid of the stuff that isn't useful, discard the ideas that aren't right. Maybe something will happen.

Glenda Jackson has frequently been accused of being intelligent. Some critics have used it as a compliment, others as an axe to hit her with. She is fearlessly frank about herself and, what is far more difficult, about some of her fellow travellers on the rickety boards that lead from one minefield of a role to another.

Glenda May Jackson is an island of mystery entirely surrounded by candour.

*   *   *

The Wirral, on the other hand, is a peninsula, a flat piece of land flanked by the estuaries of the rivers Dee and Mersey. Birkenhead, its chief town, is the place at the other end of the Mersey Tunnel. Glenda Jackson was born in a house that is no longer there in a street that has been demolished in an area that has been destroyed in order to improve the lives of its inhabitants who do not appear to be overwhelmed by gratitude. It was a place of close-packed terraced houses with front doors opening straight onto the street, unprotected by privet or garden gnome. There were chip shops and factories and grocery shops where the lentils were kept in sacks; there was a pub on every corner and, in some places, one in between for the really thirsty traveller. Life was hard but it was present and teeming.

'Now,' says Glenda Jackson, 'they've pulled everything down and there's nothing there. It's just a wasteland.'

When she was a year old the family moved to Hoylake,

once a fishing village and her father's birthplace and ancestral home. His father had been a fisherman there and Glenda's father himself had been to sea as a boy until the fishing died. He then became a bricklayer when times were good, a brick-maker when they were hard. But in the early days there was plenty of bricklaying, for the fishing village became a dormitory suburb of Birkenhead and there were big houses to be built. Glenda's mother worked too, as a barmaid and sometimes as a cleaner. There were four daughters and Glenda was the first-born, named Glenda after Glenda Farrell, an American film actress who specialised in tough girl roles and May, one of her grandmothers. It could have been Shirley after Shirley Temple, another favourite performer of her parents.

'I don't say we ever went hungry or anything like that,' Glenda says, 'but there was never any money left over.'

It was – still is – a close, warm family. 'Placid,' she told Dr Anthony Clare, a psychologist who interviewed her on BBC Radio in 1982. But 'placid' is relative, for she also told him that she and her nearest, sister, four years younger, hated each other very much and relations only became more amicable after she left home to go to drama school. There also seems to have been the usual domestic exchanges by which the mind is sharpened and the tongue turned into a deadly weapon.

She was, she told Clare, a fat, shy and acne'd youngster, given to solitary pleasures such as reading, long walks and the cinema. 'I didn't fit into the image of what girls were supposed to look like. If I'd been pretty in the accepted sense of the word, I probably wouldn't have had a career. I would just have married and settled down.'

She would, she said, have gone to the cinema every night if she had had the money. The women she admired, Bette Davis and Joan Crawford in particular, were those who 'seemed to be very capable of conducting their own lives, regardless of the dramas they had to deal with. They were not merely tough – they could be hurt but they came up smiling.'

She was, she believes, not particularly bright at school, though very disciplined; that is up to the age of 13 or 14 when she lost interest and became bored. She was at grammar school – the West Kirby Grammar School for Girls – then the traditional, indeed, the only route by which working class children could ascend to higher education. 'I wasted my last three years,' she says, 'and I never thought of going to university. I was disenchanted with the school and the whole process of learning. I was never conscious of any pressure from my family to do well, only to behave well, but there was never any thought of capitalising or using the grammar school opportunity. The sister after me went to the local secondary modern and my second sister went to grammar school like I did and the youngest went to secondary modern. And none of it made any real difference.'

There was also Sunday school until she went in for a scripture exam, won a book of Grimms' fairy tales which she already had and, as a result, never went back.

She was turned down for a number of jobs after leaving school and finally got work at Boots, the chainstore chemists, where she stayed for two years. She was, she says, bored out of her mind among the potions and lotions and eagerly accepted a friend's suggestion to join the local amateurs at the YMCA. 'It's fun,' the friend said. The first play was an Agatha Christie and she played the maid. Someone said, 'You should do this professionally.'

So she did.

'It really, truly, was a choice out of boredom. There was no self-assessment, no belief that I was cut out to be an actress or particularly fitted for the theatre, no great desire to be on the stage, certainly no belief that it was glamorous. The theatre didn't figure in anyone's thinking in my family apart from the pantomime at Christmas. Actresses were on the films.'

If her friend had introduced her to local politics instead of amateur theatre she might well, she feels, have taken up politics there and then instead of merely speaking up for the Labour Party at election times as she does here and now.

Roy Hodges, the man to whom she was married for 17 years, is said to have said: 'If she'd gone into politics she'd be prime minster; if she'd gone into crime she'd be Jack the Ripper.'

She was 18 years old and, having decided to be an actress, she wrote to the only drama school she had ever heard of, the

Royal Academy of Dramatic Art in order to get properly trained. 'I only thought as far as the next step,' she says, 'and as I now had the idea of wanting to become an actress it was clear that the first thing to do was to go to drama school. If I hadn't been accepted by RADA that, to me, would have been proof that I didn't have the ability to act. But that isn't what happened.'

She was accepted by RADA but they called her back for another audition after she told them she would have to turn down their offer because she could not afford the fees. After the second interview they wrote to the local authority to say that if they had had a scholarship she would have been given it. The local authority paid her fees for the two year course and gave her a grant sufficient for her to live on modestly. The Glenda Jackson Theatre was opened in Hoylake in 1983, the year after she was made an honorary Doctor of Literature at Liverpool University.

Glenda's family were more concerned about her leaving home for dangerous London than by her decision to become an actress. 'No one had ever moved away from home before,' she says, 'and they were very distressed to lose one. That was the really dreadful thing. We are very close-knit. But my father said, "Let her try. If it doesn't work it doesn't work and she'll come back here. But she must at least try." '

'He was always very keen that – without ever pushing us – we should have some kind of ambition, some kind of drive. They would have been happier if the drama school had been in Liverpool and they knew that acting was basically insecure. It had no reality for them. But they were very good about it and off I went.'

Home was security and Hoylake, for all the boredom of the work she did there, was a place of pleasure, a holiday resort. 'The beach was clean and the sea was clear,' she recalls, 'and I played on that beach right up to the time I left home. People used to spend their holidays in Hoylake. It's probably my fantasy that the sun always shone but it was clean and now it's dreadful. The sea is covered in yellow scrum, there's tar on the sand and the beach is a mudslide because of the pollution. There must have been stuff washed up before but now it's plastic and it doesn't break down.'

*   *   *

After a short period staying with relatives in London, Glenda moved to digs in Kew and stayed for two years in that sedate, respectable and leafy suburb.

'I led a very sheltered life,' she says, uncomplainingly. 'I would go from Kew in the mornings to drama school and then, unless there was some activity after hours, I went straight back to Kew. I really didn't know what was going on at RADA until many years later. I was totally unaware of all the subterranean currents; I didn't know about the terrible heart-rendings that were going on. Years later things would come out and I'd be amazed. I was very hard-working.'

When she says she didn't go to the theatre very often her voice signals more amazement and when she adds that she must have gone sometimes she sounds very doubtful for whatever or whoever she saw made no lasting impression on her. There could be no sense of liberation and freedom in living in London as a drama student because there had been no sense of imprisonment at home. When the holidays came she would rush back to Hoylake and work behind the counter in Woolworths and other establishments willing to take on part timers.

John Fernald, who took up his directorship of RADA the term that Glenda started, was noted for his practical attitude to the theatre. His parting advice to her when she left at the age of 21 was, 'Don't expect much work before you're 40. Essentially, you're a character actress.'

But by the time she left RADA Glenda had an agent, not at all an easy acquisition for newcomers as agents generally conclude that ten per cent of nothing doesn't cover postage and telephone calls.

'I was in one of the public shows at the end of my last term,' says Glenda, 'and out of that I got an agent, Crouch, and out of that I got a job, very quickly, at Worthing rep.'

She was at Worthing for two months, playing in *Separate Tables* and *Doctor in the House* and then, she confided to Pamela Harvey who interviewed her for Clive Swift's career guide, *The Performing World of the Actor*★ she was 'deeply distressed because they didn't ask me to stay and become a permanent member of the company.'

Peter Crouch, still her agent after 26 years, recalls that the first time he saw Glenda in a RADA production he noted her as being 'very interesting.' Then he saw her as Eliza in *Pygmalion*. 'That convinced me that here was someone who was quite extraordinary,' he says.

'I was sitting next to another agent, now retired, who always took cucumber sandwiches to RADA end-of-term productions. Between munches he asked, 'Who are you looking at?"

' "That girl playing Eliza."

' "You'll never sell her to the Rank Organisation."

' "Hopefully not," I said. I never looked on Glenda as someone who was immediately going to go into movies, much less into the Rank Charm School.★

'I never thought she was going to be the easiest actress to promote. She has an individual quality which I reckoned was not going to appeal to everybody. But there is an enormous sex appeal. Something exudes from her like it does from a very healthy animal. She hasn't a high opinion of her own physical attractions. She once told me, 'I don't know why I keep getting all these scripts with nude scenes. I've got varicose veins, piano legs and no tits."

'But the camera falls in love with her. A lighting cameraman once told me it was because she had "wonderful lighting about the eyes" by which it turned out that he meant she had high cheek bones. So forget the ski-run nose and the snaggle tooth; the eyes are the things that matter in films.'

But before the days of the cameramen were the years of hardship. There was work for a time. Worthing was followed

---

★ Hamish Hamilton, London, 1981

★ The Rank Charm School was set up by the Rank Film Organisation to groom attractive girls and train them in opening garden parties and attending film premieres. They were called starlets, though few ever became stars. Charm went out of fashion in the early 'sixties.

by Hornchurch and a first West End appearance at the Arts Theatre in 1957 in a play called *All Kinds of Men*. She was invited to join the newly-re-opened repertory theatre at Crewe and spent six months there playing minor roles and assisting with stage management. The stage manager was Roy Hodges and they eventually married. After Crewe Glenda went on tour in *A Girl Called Sadie* in which she played a grandma in a cotton-wool wig. This play mercifully seems to have disappeared from the annals of 20th century theatre and Glenda herself can remember nothing about it except that it was terrible.

That was bad enough; worse was to come – two years without any theatre work at all. She found occasional jobs as shop assistant, waitress, switchboard operator (for a time at Crouch's agency). 'You get quite good at lying when you apply for a job like that,' she has said, 'pretending that you will stay for the rest of your life. My parents went through all that terrible agony of seeing me being more out of work than in and going home with holes in my shoes. It was very hard for them,' she told Pamela Harvey. 'It was soul-destroying for me.'

But it did not occur to her, even at the blackest times, that she was in the wrong business. How could it when she had never been given the opportunity to prove that she could be what she said she was – an actress?

'That was the worst time,' she says, 'though I'd take anything – all the odds and sods I could get. Two years of rejection! I hate auditions.'

She told Pamela Harvey: 'Every time they had auditions for the Royal Shakespeare Company I would be sent along and do my little piece. I never got any work from it. They're crucifying. You can tell absolutely nothing from an audition which is what is so painful. You go along prepared to act and all they're looking at is your height, your weight, your colour and whether you fit into the scheme of things. Nobody looks at you as a human being or a person. You feel like a beggar and all you want to do is work.'

Crouch says that he sent her twice to auditions at the RSC and that she was twice turned down. Years later he was shown Peter Hall's note on her. It read: 'Interesting, but a bit rich for our blood.'

*　　*　　*

But work started to come in more regularly and after *The Idiot* at Hammersmith came Bill Naughton's *Alfie* with John Neville at the Mermaid. Glenda played Siddie, one of the girls in Alfie's lusty life. 'She is right at the beginning and right at the end. He's having it off with her in the back of the car. She's just one of his regular, occasional ladies,' is how she describes the role. A month later, in July, 1964, the production transferred to the Duchess Theatre. There she was seen by Charles Marowitz, a young American who had worked as Peter Brook's assistant director on the Scofield *King Lear* at Stratford-on-Avon the year before and who eventually was to start his own experimental theatre, the Open Space, which was, in fact, a claustrophobic basement in Tottenham Court Road.

Marowitz, a tall bearded New Yorker with a sense of mission made a considerable impact on the British theatre, though not as much as he would have wished. Not, it must be hastily added, for egotistical reason – though ego is not absent – but because he was convinced – and probably still is though he is now teaching in California – that the British theatre was in dire need of revitalization. This was mainly to be achieved through the implementation of the theories of Antonin Artaud (1896–1948), described by Martin Esslin in his book, *Theatre of the Absurd** as 'one of the most extraordinary men of his age, actor, director, prophet, blasphemer, saint, madman and a great poet . . . (whose) vision of a stage of magic, beauty and mythical power remains to this day one of the most active leavens in the theatre.'

Towards the end of 1963, Peter Brook and Marowitz, backed by the Royal Shakespeare Company, then still under the direction of Peter Hall, set up what Marowitz himself

---

* Eyre and Spottiswoode, 1962.

19

was to describe as a 'curious' experimental season called 'The Theatre of Cruelty'. They were to operate at LAMDA, the London Academy of Music and Dramatic Art, in Kensington and their intention was to explore certain problems of acting and stagecraft in laboratory conditions without the commercial pressures of public performance. They wanted actors who were 'open, adaptable and ready to rush in where rigid pros feared to tread.'*

In order to find these actors they devised a different kind of audition. Instead of giving individual readings actors were asked to work together for at least an hour in groups of eight to ten. But at first the actor was asked to perform his two-minute set piece without any suggestion or interference. Then he was given a new character and a new situation and asked to play his original text in the new circumstances. Then, still using the same text, he was asked to transform himself into a market huckster or a political candidate seeking re-election. Then he was given cue words relating to each character and required to switch from one to another without breaking the flow of the original text.

'There were,' says Marowitz drily, 'many more equally destabilising exercises.'

Out of the first 50 actors auditioned twelve were selected and presented to Brook for approval. He had doubts about only one, Glenda Jackson. As far as Glenda was concerned all that happened was that there was a pause between her first and second auditions. Her set piece was a Dorothy Parker story.

'I did it and then Brook said, "Now do it as a woman who's been taken away to a lunatic asylum and has been put into a straitjacket." And then he added, "But she isn't, in fact, mad." '

'I had never been asked to do anything like that in my life, so I did it. And then I didn't hear anything for a time

---

* *Theatre at Work: Playwrights and Productions in the Modern British Theatre*, Edited by Charles Marowitz and Simon Trussler, Methuen & Co., London, 1967.

Rehearsing for *Hamlet* with David Warner, Stratford-on-Avon. *Photo*: Gordon Goode.

and then I had to go back and do another audition and this time there were four of us and Marowitz and Brook. Brook did most of the talking and then I didn't hear anything more for a time and then I was told I was one of the twelve, one of the chosen. Years later I asked Marowitz "why?" and he said it was a toss up between me and somebody else but that he had pushed for me. Which I think is probably the truth.'

Marowitz, writing in the New York Times magazine in January, 1975, said: 'Glenda Jackson was nose-to-nose with an odds-on favourite for the final place. I found myself mounting a frantic campaign for her to be chosen.

'My fervour was so uncharacteristic that Brook wondered if I had sexual designs on the girl. I assured him that wasn't the case and, when asked to state my reasons, found myself explaining tamely that she was beautifully screwed up and that during a four-hour audition workout I had developed the impression that she was, in some inexplicable way, mined. I remember the very first interview I had with her in some woebegone room (an almost obligatory setting for rehearsals in England), watching her stark nutty eyes shifting slowly in her head like arc-lights; feeling that behind that studied stillness was a cobra ready to spring or a hysteric ready to break down; choosing my words carefully and getting back short, orderly answers that betrayed the very minimum both of feeling and information; perpetually conscious of a smouldering intelligence rating both my questions and her own answers as she shifted her focus from within to without, suggesting the mechanism of a hypersensitive tape recorder that could fast-forward or re-wind with the flick of an invisible switch. I had no way of knowing at the time that banked up behind that interview were two years of anguished unemployment and the soul-destroying poverty that imposes. I was aware only of a disconcerting presence; something inaudibly but palpably ticking; something capable of "going off." '

Glenda remembers it slightly differently. 'It was the most important job of my life,' she says, 'but I didn't know it at the time. It was the kind of work I'd always imagined must exist somewhere, but which I'd never come across, so when I got it I was thrilled by it. But at the time I didn't think it was crucial that I got the job. In fact I didn't expect to get it because I'd never got a job through an audition in my life. And, anyway, I was going quite well, work was beginning to come in fairly regularly. But I'd seen a couple of Brook's productions and I thought he was wonderful director and his theories which I knew and which, in fact, are practical realities, had no place in the theatre I was working in at the time.

'We worked for about three months and it was incredible, like coming across an oasis in the desert.'

Clearly not the Oscar-winning film roles, the acclaim of theatre audiences in London and New York, certainly not the glitter of a life which, for all her rejection of glamour, has had its share of the shallower excitements as well as the deeper satisfactions, could outglow the remembered joy of those three austere and intensive months of work with Brook when, without spectators or other pressures, the acting identity of Glenda Jackson was shaped and defined; for whatever it was that went into that crucible, something different came out.

One of the reasons for the Royal Shakespeare Company's interest in the Theatre of Cruelty was that they planned to stage Genet's *The Screens* (*Les Paravents*), written in 1961 and, ostensibly, a satire on the Algerian War. It needs a huge cast and Genet demands that the play be performed in the open air on four levels and in front of a wide variety of screens. There are about 100 characters and Genet needs hardly to insist, as he does, that each actor must play five or six roles. The action takes place in an Arab village among the very poorest people. The poorest of all is Said and, therefore, he can only marry the ugliest girl. It contains what Esslin describes as 'a profusion of images of anal eroticism.'

In an interview at the time, *Brook and Marowitz discussed their aims and methods with Simon Trussler. Marowitz said that *The Screens* would simply not work with the bland British approach to acting; 'it requires a kind of depth approach that has to be first learnt and developed in actors and only after the experience has been *had* can it then

---

* *Plays and Players*, February, 1964

be applied to the play. What we are trying to do at this stage is to create such an instrument using these 10 or 12 actors which, once it is developed, will be able to grapple with the play. . . .

'We're . . . exploring certain areas which have not yet been explored and which through exploration might yield a different type of acting and theatrical result. It might conceivably shake up other people and give them certain directions.'

Brook said: 'There are very few actors anywhere in the world qualified to understand how, within a virtually naturalistic framework which passes at times into what one can call an epic framework, there can suddenly take place an Artaud-like ceremony. Few actors exist who can take that in their stride and certainly no group of actors each one understanding what the others are doing and being able to respond in shifting styles. . . . We are trying to put the actor in situations where, for instance, he has to take his first impulse and turn it maybe into pure sound like an Artaud cry, maybe into formal gesture, maybe into a leap, maybe (as in *The Screens* itself) into rushing up to a sheet of white paper and attacking it with paint. What we are *trying* to bring about is for the actor, in making his choice, to make it as an independent, responsible, creative artist . . .

'We hope to weld the group of actors into a special sort of fighting force. Our main hope in this particular experiment is that it will have the right sort of provocative *professional* effect – and this is different to what Artaud was doing. His aim was infinitely larger and would relate to something that we can't attempt to get to at once, which was to have that effect on *life*.'

Eleven years later, Marowitz wrote * that there were 'interminable improvisations and games in which the actor's personal imagination was being constantly nudged, wooed or flagellated into action. In circumstances such as these one sees the centrifugal talent of each person in clear, unmistakeable terms. Glenda's choices were staggering. Invariably unex-

---

* *New York Times* magazine article.

pected, often tinged with sarcasm or perversity, occasionally droll with a hard, urban kind of humour which was three-quarters irony and one-quarter absurdity, a complete sensibility spiralling up out of the labyrinthine depths.'

Marowitz says that one of the actors complained that Glenda was destructive and negative, but what he was really saying, according to Marowitz, was that Glenda radiated disgust in those days, but its object was the sloppy, ill-defined, unthought-out mugging which passed for acting in the English theatre and, particularly, the appearance of those characteristics in herself. 'Whenever she worked one could hear her built-in bull detector, that most delicate of all precision instruments, ticking in the background and the actors who resented her most were those whose execrable effusions were being scrutinised and judged in the glare of those cold, sleepy, cruel eyes.'

Marowitz tends to become excitable in prose; Glenda remains prosaic, the flat North of England vowels not lending themselves to extravagant interpretations.

'It was a series of exercises of one kind or another,' is how she recalls those stirring times. 'I remember that one day we had to throw paint at sheets of white paper.'

Marowitz has vivid memories of her 'lounging around the rehearsal room looking like a scrubwoman, her face not only un-made up but seemingly scrubbed raw as if to obliterate her features, emitting great waves of langour tinged with ennui; a softly pulsating indictment of everything crude, crummy and unworthy in our work.'

Glenda says: 'That was the best work I've ever done. It was very exciting.'

Brook decided that the three months of work needed some kind of focus and, besides, there was much curiosity about what had been going on at LAMDA. A revue was created and presented in January, 1964. It included Artaud's surrealist sketch, *A Spurt of Blood*, presented both in the original text and then entirely in screams, sketches by Robbe-Grillet, Paul Ableman, John Arden and Brook and two collages created by Marowitz and Brook out of Marowitz's Hamlet Variation, a shortened version of the play in which Marowitz sets out to deride 'the supreme prototype of the conscience-stricken but paralysed liberal, one of the most lethal and obnoxious characters in modern times.'*

Brook called the evening a public work-in-progress session, a form of surrealist revue composed of shots in the dark, shots at distant targets. 'We are,' he said, 'exploring theatre language . . . there are no rules any more.'

The item that made the biggest impact was created by Brook himself. It involved Glenda being stripped, bathed and dressed in a prison uniform to the words of a report on the Christine Keeler case. The same words were then used as she was transformed into Jackie Kennedy at the President's funeral.

Christine Keeler was a young woman whose bedtime involvements with both the British Defence Minister, John Profumo, and a Soviet naval attaché, led to the former's resignation and subsequent immersion in social work in London's East End. Christine Keeler endured or enjoyed several years of notoriety which are not entirely over and the Soviet sailor passed into Soviet obscurity. It was never seriously supposed that Profumo had passed on any secrets to Keeler but it served as a mole-hill on which to build a mountain of hypocrisy.

Jackie Kennedy widow of the assassinated President, John Kennedy, was regarded by many as a supreme example of the finest kind of woman and was beautiful and intelligent to boot. Nowadays it would seem an intolerable act of presumption towards both women to cast them at opposing ends of some notional scale of virtue which, one suspects, had less to do with sexual morality than with style. That is to say that Jackie Kennedy wore classier clothes, knew more writers and had a better taste in music than Christine Keeler. Still, in the middle sixties, the concept seemed to have some validity.

It was not a public performance, the audience all being there by invitation only. As a result it did not come under the authority of the Lord Chamberlain whose business it was to ban words, scenes and sometimes whole plays that he deemed would offend against public morality or something.

---

* *The Marowitz Shakespeare*, Marion Boyars, 1978

Photo oppostie: Glenda dancing in *Women in Love.*

All the same, this was the first time a serious actress had fully disrobed in a serious cause in public * and those who were present took it very seriously indeed. Not sure how we should react, we took refuge in perfect stillness. A fidget could have been misinterpreted, a cough would have been uncool, a laugh would have had us drummed out of the pages of 'Plays and Players.'

Marowitz recalls: 'Before it came to the final stripping rehearsals, I remember that Peter and I wondered whether the actress would refuse. . . . When it came to the delicate, last day rehearsals and the stripping had to be rehearsed. I remember Glenda's dry, undramatic resignation – accepting not the embarrassment of appearing nude, but the necessity of the act in regard to the play. Whatever convoluted thought-processes and emotional wrenching may have paved the way, the decision itself, like everything else in her life, was brisk, clear and decisive. It was the role, not her directors which had persuaded her, and that was the only authority she ever obeyed implicitly.'

Sitting in the second row of the LAMDA theatre, her agent, Peter Crouch, wondered if she was embarrassed. 'Then,' he says, 'I forgot that thought the moment she started acting. Nobody in the audience was embarrassed in the slightest.'

Janet Suzman, an actress who has worked with her, not talking particularly about this event, says: 'The thing about Glenda is that she has no sense of shame; and I mean that admiringly. She feels that she has nothing to be ashamed about. She accepts herself entirely as she is and expects others to do the same.'

And how did Glenda feel at the time? 'Cold,' she says. 'It was very chilly. That's the only thing that worried me. Essentially, Brook's interest was in discovering the potential in a kind of ritual theatre, but there were lots of other

---

* We thought so then but theatre historians (the late) Ray Mander and Joe Mitchenson say that the first was Peggy Ashcroft in a club performance of *Fraulein Elsa* at the Kingsway Theatre in 1932.

influences that were being brought to bear. The only time I've ever really felt utterly inhibited in an acting sense was when we were doing *US* and we had to go off the stage and into the audience. I need that fourth wall. If the stripping had been in another context, I don't know whether I would have worried about it, but I was certainly not worried at the time. There was also the fact that we had all been working together for three months, very intense work, and there is a curious kind of intimacy that actors have among themselves which is specific entirely to the work. By that I mean that on an acting level you can quite easily break through all those social barriers that keep the world spinning and then have absolutely nothing to say to each other once the work has stopped. The audience did not worry me at all, only on the level that I hoped they would understand what we were doing.'

They never did perform Genet's *The Screens*, except partially and in a half-hearted way at the Donmar Rehearsal Theatre.

'Brook had got bored with the idea of doing it,' says Glenda, 'and he came back from Germany with another play which was going to be put on by the Royal Shakespeare Company at the Aldwych Theatre, so we were all employed by the RSC in the main group.'

The play Brook had seen in Germany was *The Persecution and Assassination of Marat as Performed by the Inmates of the Asylum of Charenton under the Direction of the Marquis de Sade*. It was to be known thereafter as the *Marat/Sade*. It was one of a pair of Brook productions for the RSC, the other being *US*, which stood for both the United States and us, which, in retrospect, seem to typify much of that peculiar combination of performance and politics that developed in the 'sixties and was a major contribution to the character of the decade.

'Working with Brook on these two productions in particular,' says Glenda, 'my belief that the whole is greater than the sum of the parts was practically applied. Everybody was responsible for the whole production, not just for their little piece of the action. Those two productions crystalised my attitudes and ideas about what is best in a theatrical sense and that, in turn, extends into what I regard as being best in a social context. I'm not interested in theatre that is merely a spectator sport. The most exciting and, to me, the only valid reason for having a theatre is that, upon occasions, you can create a microcosm of an ideal society. The energy created on the stage passes into the audience, is increased by the energy of the audience, and passes back. When that happens there is a real sense of bonding, of sharing, of being a unit and what the actors do is enhanced by what the audience do.

'I don't think any major changes are brought about in the blinking of an eye. It can happen for individuals occasionally, but I don't think that's the point for me. Theatre can and should hold the mirror up to ourselves in the hope that we will dislike the reflection sufficiently to wish to change it, or else to show an image which is so desirable that we would wish to become it. But, essentially, my social view of the purpose of the theatre in any society that wishes to consider itself well-balanced and productive – as opposed to being decadent and hanging on by its finger nails – is to provide the shared experience, that extraordinary coming together of a group of strangers who watch another group of strangers and, by that act, lose their strangeness. It may last no longer than it takes you to walk through an exit door, but that experience when it happens is undeniable and that, as an idea of what it is to be a human being in the company of other human beings, is very valuable.'

She did not come by her politics through any particular revelation or injustice on the road from Hoylake to Hollywood. Nor did she inherit it. Indeed, she believes that her family, though clearly working class, regularly voted for Selwyn Lloyd (a Conservative Foreign Secretary and Chancellor of the Exchequer in the Macmillan administration) who was the Member of Parliament for Wirral for the whole of his considerable political career.

'My politics,' she said, 'came by a process of osmosis. I absorbed the views of all the writers I read and though I started in the public library at A and went on to Z, all the writers I've been most interested in and those I return to again and again are people who have exposed the iniquities of society. Oddly enough, a lot of them are Americans. Shaw? I read him for his plays as much as anything else. Dos Passos made a big impression on me and the early Sinclair Lewis; Howard Fast, Steinbeck, Thomas Wolfe – all of them writers who dealt with the social realities of their time. Among British writers Lawrence and, of course, Orwell. Jane Austen too, though I came late to her. She's a marvellous social commentator. But apart from Sartre and Gide I didn't read any Europeans until much later.*

'I suppose I'm middle-of-the-road Left. It's partly because I'd like my side to win and you're never going to win anything in England if you opt for an extreme. Anyway, the extremes of Right and Left invariably come out the same, quite apart from sounding the same. There comes a point when, if you're really going to be truthful about your extreme views, you have to accommodate the use of violence. And I will certainly not accept the use of violence for a political end, certainly not in a country like Britain.

'My attitude to work is linked very directly with my political thinking, muddled and limited though it may be. It doesn't apply so much to the content of what I do, mainly because I've never read a really good fascist play. But the theatre has to be open to every kind of thought. Where I draw the line is where the thinking takes the place of good work. The message is not enough. It would be marvellous if you could find a play that totally supported your political views, but in a way it's irrelevant because what is really important is the *way* you work. That is the strongest political message – that you work in a way that supports your views about how society itself should run.'

Her first broadly political play was the *Marat/Sade* in which she played Charlotte Corday who murdered Marat by sticking a knife into him while he was taking a bath. Or rather she played the inmate of an asylum who played Charlotte Corday.

There was madness in the Theatre of Cruelty, madness

---

* She uses 'Europeans' as most British people do, to mean those who live on the continent of Europe'.

in the *Marat/Sade* and, a short time afterwards, madness as Ophelia in the Stratford-on-Avon production of *Hamlet* in which David Warner played the prince.

'Too much importance must not be attached to this,' says Glenda firmly. 'Acting isn't being. When we were doing the *Marat/Sade* we spent weeks and weeks not working on the text but trying to define what insanity is. Is it divine? Is the madman the only sane person?

'Brook would say, "Right, tell me about someone you know who is insane." And people would say, "Well, I heard . . ." But Brook would interrupt and say, "I don't want to know what you've heard; I want to know what you've actually seen."

'He took a lot of them to lunatic asylums. I never went. Nowadays, of course, it would be irrelevant because everybody's sedated. The one thing that came out is that insanity extends nothing; an insane person walks a very narrow line and does it with constant repetition. To discover a thing like that is very valuable for an actor. The way into a performance is to get a fact which releases the imagination. You then do as much as is within your grasp and hope that there's something there.'

Brook made them study paintings by Breughel and Hogarth and etchings by Goya. They watched two French films, *Regard sur la Folie* and *Le Maitre-Fous*. Brook told his company that they must 'dig out' the madness in themselves and find personal expressions of madness that were not only true but could be sustained for two and a half hours.

'We were,' said Glenda shortly afterwards, 'all convinced that we were going loony.'

Glenda's Charlotte was a somnambulistic lunatic with an intensity of expression so icily innocent, so unmarked by human experience, that it chilled the heart.

The play's concern was a debate between authority, as exemplified by Marat (Clive Revill), proponent of the utilitarian authoritarian state, and freedom, as expressed by de Sade (Patrick Magee), voluptuary, anarch and champion of unbridled individual liberty. Though still studied at universities, it is perhaps significant that the play has never been revived, in

Gudrun (Glenda Jackson) and Ursula (Jennie Linden) in *Women in Love*.

Britain at least.

'It's a very unfair play,' says Glenda. 'Peter Weiss, the author, thought of it as a strong political document and perhaps for him it was. But for me it isn't, because Marat never really comes up with an argument as convincing as de Sade's because de Sade simply puts the case for humanity and humanism, for instinct and response against what seems to be a debilitating and restrictive order. But if you really examine the arguments you can drive a coach and horses through both of them – Marat's more easily than de Sade's. So on that level it doesn't have a great deal of credibility, but it was very much part of that seeming political energy of the time. It was Brook's production that was important. I don't think there's a lot in the play itself, but there was at the time and that tells you more about the time than about the play.'

If anything, *US* – Glenda, ever precise, defuses its ambiguity by nearly always referring to it as U.S. – 'Us' – says even more about the times. But between the *Marat/Sade* and *US* there was the 1965 Stratford-on-Avon season in which Glenda played the Princess of France in *Love's Labour's Lost* and Ophelia in *Hamlet* in which she went mad on the stage and, she says, had her sanity saved by one review of her performance.

Prince of Stratford

'As I was in the company they had to use me,' says Glenda. 'And I also had a strong feeling that I should do Shakespeare. Equally, I can remember how my heart sank when I knew what plays they were doing that season. I have no natural sympathy for Ophelia or the Princess of France. I never think I have any natural feeling for playing Shakespeare until I actually come to do it. And then – well, you can't back off from it, can you?

'With Ophelia I did what I always do when I come to a part – I read the play several times just straight through, not looking to see who's what or where anything is – I just read it. The work is done at rehearsals; work happens with other people. I don't go in with a performance ready or even an idea ready and complete. I may have ideas, but they have to be tossed up in the air and seen in relation to other people's ideas.

'As far as Ophelia is concerned I don't believe she is weak. Weak people don't break, they bend. It's only the seemingly strong people who snap and there's nothing in the play to lead you to believe that before her madness Ophelia is regarded as so sensitive a flower that she will go over the edge at the slightest push. So the madness has to come as a surprise to everybody. And it can only come as a surprise if, up to that point, she seems to have her balance. So that was where I worked from.

'But that's one of the remarkable things about Shakespeare – he is such a consummate writer that you can practically make any theory fit. There didn't seem to be anything in the text that made my view of Ophelia all that difficult to maintain. I do think the clash between her emotions about Hamlet and her feelings about her father produce the kind of friction that makes that kind of insanity possible. That was the reasoning behind my performance.

'If you stand up for your belief, Peter Hall's one of those

35

directors who tends to back off a little. Anyway, from a director's point of view, *Hamlet* is very much Hamlet and that's where his focus was. I have to say I don't regard Peter Hall highly as a director and, therefore, I wasn't really looking for inspiration or guidance from him. I expected him to be pretty much as he turned out to be.

'What happened was very interesting. We opened midweek and I read the notices and I thought, "Well, I've gone mad. What they see isn't what I'm doing, but as everyone's seeing it, I've lost touch with what I'm doing and what I think I'm doing I'm really not doing. I've really gone mad." It was a very curious sensation.

'And then the Sundays came out and Penelope Gilliatt in *The Observer* had actually seen what I was doing and it restored my faith in myself. I hadn't had some kind of nervous breakdown. It was quite extraordinary.'

'Ophelia, as played by Glenda Jackson, is a new character altogether in my experience, a brisk young lady of the court, entirely sophisticated and with all her wits so much about her that it is absurd to think that she could credibly lose them.' – W.A. Darlington, *Daily Telegraph*.

'. . . . tough, confident . . . with one of those voices that sounds as if she were trying to make herself heard on a bad telephone. From such a start pathos is impossible to achieve in her insanity; and her decision to accompany her mad songs on the lute alienates our sympathies still more since she seems to be perfectly well in command of everything else she is doing.' – B.A. Young, *Financial Times*.

'An eccentric Glenda Jackson, who barks her lines and croaks the mad songs to her own lute accompaniment,' – *The Times* (unsigned, but almost certainly Victor Cookman).

'Clearly this Hamlet would not be attracted by anything from Roedean or even Heathfield.* His cup of tea would have prussic acid in it. Glenda Jackson is given a harsh, bitter, setting-teeth-on-edge recipe for Ophelia and loyally cooks according to the specification.' – Harold Hobson, *Sunday Times*.

---

* Two expensive English public (that is private) schools for girls.

Glenda with her son Daniel,
mother and Oscar, 1971.

'Glenda Jackson's quacking deb of an Ophelia, shrill in her aggression, dangerous in her anger, is a Chelsea-set beatnik who could swap obscenities any night. She seems more likely to smoke pot than go potty at her father's death.' – Alan Brien, *Sunday Telegraph*.

But in *The Observer*, under a four-column heading, 'Ophelia, Prince of Stratford,' Penelope Gilliatt wrote:

'Glenda Jackson is the first Ophelia I have seen who should play Hamlet. In Peter Hall's production of the play at Stratford she has all the qualities of a great prince. She makes Ophelia exceptional and electric, with an intelligence that harasses the court and a scornful authority full of Hamlet's own self-distaste.

'When she says, "Pray you, mark" to the twittering Gertrude in the mad scene she shouts the words as though she could do murder, drumming a heel on the floor and lifting her upper lip in a rictus of contempt. The speech when she is alone after 'Get thee to a nunnery' is jagged with pain; 'blasted with ecstasy' is hideously screeched, not bleated, and the mood is spiked with suicidal sarcasm.

'In Peter Hall's specifically social production, where Hamlet's chief disability is that he cannot connect, the performance stands out extraordinarily. It is full of rancour and fiercely unsentimental, the only Ophelia I have ever seen that has the real, shrivelled, shrewish roots of madness. It is executed with the sort of attack that is usually thought of as a quality of male acting, much more so than Hamlet himself.

'Maybe this is deliberate. When a production places the play so firmly in the world of the cool, politically disaffected generation, one of the first things that will result is a modern blurring of the sexual boundaries.'

And I for one, who wrote * that Glenda Jackson's Ophelia was the fiercest I had ever seen, more likely to institute an action for breach of promise than commit suicide, am prepared to acknowledge Penelope Gilliatt's perception and insight with

---

* *The Sun*, April 20, 1965. (The Odhams/IPC 'Sun', not the present Murdoch 'Sun').

a couple of reservations. The first is that, as Kathryn Pogson proved in a recent Jonathan Miller production of *Hamlet*, Ophelia can equally be played as a girl who is on the edge of a clinically recognisable psychosis from the start. It is also possible to argue that the last thing *Hamlet* needs is an Ophelia who could play the prince.

Years later, Penelope Gilliatt wrote the film, *Sunday Bloody Sunday* which brought Glenda the best actress award from the British Film Academy.

Seventeen years after those lacerating Ophelia reviews, objectivity is returning.

'What is interesting,' Glenda says, 'is that there can be a universal acceptance by people of something that is utterly different from your intention, or indeed, what you are actually doing. That's why Shakespeare is a genius because he writes about how people really are and not how we would like to think they are. In truth, we make assessments of people and take them as being absolute, even though we should know that what we know is only what we see. Certainly, so far as Ophelia is concerned, in the society in which she was functioning nothing had happened to deflect anybody's opinion of her as being other than she seemed. What you and the others said is that what you had seen of Ophelia had led you to expect her to react in a certain way which is like future-telling. What is marvellous about Shakespeare, and what is true, is that however much you may think you know somebody you don't. And if a certain situation arises in a woman's life at a certain age and in a certain emotional climate and she is in an emotional state, she cannot actually deal with it. But if she had the ability to react by bringing a breach of promise action then Shakespeare would have written her differently. Perhaps as Lady Macbeth, though she and Ophelia share that element of believing that they can cope with a situation and then find, when they are actually in it, that they can't.'

Glenda made her New York debut at the Martin Beck Theatre in December, 1965 in *Marat/Sade* and in October, 1966, after months of preparation, returned to the Aldwych stage with a major role in *US*, a partly-scripted, partly-devised howl of protest at the Vietnam War.

Programme note by Brook: 'This performance is a collaboration. We have attempted together to understand a situation too vast to encompass alone and too painful to ignore. A programme is the place in which, conventionally, credit must be given where it is due. In this case, any division of responsibilities is conventional, not precise.'

Programme note by L.T.G. Farmer, Chairman of the Executive Council of the Royal Shakespeare Company: 'The Executive Council of the Royal Shakespeare Theatre firmly believes that it has a duty to support the company's presentation of serious experimental work, however controversial, whilst, of course, not agreeing individually or collectively with all the views expressed.

'Documentary drama as yet in its infancy, may well prove able to challenge people to serious thought over burning topical problems more forcefully than newspapers, radio or television.

'*US* is an attempt by a body of dedicated people – directors, writers, actors and designers – to pass balanced comment in a responsible way on a current problem of vital concern to all.'

This should not be read as an attempt by the RSC's executive council to evade or shift responsibility for the production. J. C. Trewin in his biography of Peter Brook * says that Farmer, Peter Hall and Brook went to St James's Palace to see the Lord Chamberlain, Lord Cobbold, who thought that the script for *US* was 'bestial, anti-American and communist.' He had already asked Farmer to exercise his influence and prevent it from being staged. On the contrary, Farmer, after seeing a rehearsal, insisted that it was a performance of integrity and in no sense easily propagandist. It was not anti-American, he said, though it was critical of Britain and the USA.

The Lord Chamberlain asked: 'If the American Ambassador should come to the first night would he walk out?'

---

* Macdonald, 1971.

'No,' said Farmer, 'not if he stayed until the end.'

This Marx Brothers exchange clearly comforted Lord Cobbold for his doubts were allayed and he issued a licence for the play to be performed.

'Vietnam,' says Glenda, 'was the only topic in anybody's mind at the time and the basic reason for doing '*US*-Us' was that we wanted to find a way of theatrically entering into the debate. What was there in the theatrical armoury that could illuminate, examine and probe the situation? How could one's theatrical craft be brought to bear? It started out with the bulk of the people involved in it being fiercely and vehemently anti-American. Brook was not one of them. As far as he was concerned it wasn't an exercise in knocking America.'

They worked on it for 17 weeks before it reached the stage and seven of those weeks were without any kind of script. All they had was factual material and they were inundated by it. They were trying to devise something that reflected the British attitude to the war in Vietnam. Eventually, playwright and ex-actor Denis Cannan joined the company and wrote a three-act play which was condensed to form the second half of the production.

Before the interval, in an episode which was later to be abandoned, the actors, brown paper bags over their heads, stumbled into the audience, apparently to test the bourgeoisie's sympathy for the helpless victims of war. It is as if the actors supposed that the audience could not tell the difference between a wounded Vietnamese and an actor stumbling about with a paper bag over his head. This was when, to Glenda's discomfort, the fourth wall was temporarily abolished.

She made a speech in which she prayed with fervour that firebombs would rain down on an English suburban lawn and the irreverent thought crossed some minds that some twenty years earlier that was precisely what had happened. The evening ended with the apparent burning of a white butterfly as a symbol of the fires that had consumed so many of the Vietnamese. Then the house lights went up, the actors lined up and they and the audience stared at each other. Brook wrote in *The Times* two years later that, at this point, the actors were 'switching their attention to a private task in which

41

As Nina in *The Music Lovers*.

they evaluated their own personal views in the light of the day's events and the evening's performance.' No one knew this at the time, of course, and Kenneth Tynan, literary manager of the National Theatre, eventually demanded in a loud voice: 'Are you waiting for us, or are we waiting for you?'

Despite reservations, the evening had enormous theatrical vitality and an undeniable integrity. There were some, however, who thought it cheap and facile.

'The strongest criticism we faced,' says Glenda, 'was that it was not sufficiently anti-American. Night after night, someone in the auditorium would say something and the debate would take off. There were many evenings when we would leave the theatre and the audience were still there, arguing. In a way there was an awful responsibility. One night a young girl came to my dressing room in a state of total emotional breakdown. She was crying and couldn't speak and stood there, shaking. She was looking to me for some kind of restitution of her equilibrium that we had destroyed or distorted and there was absolutely nothing I could do except get her a taxi and hope she'd get home. The truth of it was that all I was really concerned with was (a) getting a drink because I was so parched by the end of the second act and (b) getting myself home. And that aspect of it, which I suppose was the area we really should have been examining, was not touched on.'

Glenda made her film debut directed by Brook in the *Marat/Sade* and followed it up with a movie version of *US* re-titled *Tell Me Lies* which does not seem to have been seen by more than half a dozen people. She worked with him again in the theatre in 1968, at first in Paris which, ironically, they were forced to leave because of the student revolution. They took refuge at the Round House in London. Brook was directing her in a small role in *The Tempest*. She was to have played one of the masque goddesses she calls Snap, Crackle and Pop, not inappropriately as she would have been Ceres. But she fell ill a week before the opening and was replaced. The next time she and Brook worked together was in 1978 when she played Cleopatra at Stratford-on-Avon.

He has had incalculable influence on the kind of actress

she is, but she would have been remarkable whatever company she had kept, for the intelligence and drive belong to her alone.

'Some actors go towards the parts and transform themselves into them, becoming the characters they play,' says Janet Suzman. 'Glenda draws the role towards her and it becomes her with her silhouette, her persona. But it is the character all the same.'

'All acting,' Glenda says, 'involves drawing on yourself at one level but you do not necessarily have to have experienced the situation you are playing. Or have felt the same emotion. What you have to try to find is an equivalent emotional situation that is valid for you. One of the difficulties is when you do something that requires more than realism or naturalism. That's when having worked with Brook is very valuable, for you can go at something obliquely and find the additional dimensions you need within it. Lots of times to be utterly realistic or naturalistic doesn't begin to meet the needs of the play. In Shakespeare, for instance, it's not so much a problem between the actress and the role as between the actress and the acting. It's nothing specific to a particular part, for each part makes its own particular demands. But there's certainly a link between the person and the attitude to the work. The trouble is that words are so imprecise. The analogy, even though it is a completely different art form – and not, in one way, as great – is music. I don't think anyone would say to interpreters of music that it was their personal experiences that made it possible for them to be particularly good because life is more than what you actually experience. What is interesting are the possibilities and that's what I think acting is about. If you gave Romeo and Juliet to two 14-year-olds who were actually in love it would be the most boring evening you've ever spent in the theatre.

'No, it's got nothing to do with their lack of technique; it's got a lot to do with what you're looking for – which is the essence of something, a distillation of experience, something that a group of people can react to. If you make it entirely specific at the only level of experience available to you then it is only meaningful to you. So you have to find out what is true of that experience for everybody and what is true is hardly ever the externals. So how do you find it? You may use your experience as part of the way in, but it's not the sum total.'

One of the key factors is energy.

'It's energy that makes all the difference between a live and a dead performance,' she says. 'It's the thing the Chinese have of being able to fill everything with absolute energy. Look at their martial arts. All of them are based on their philosophy of absolute giving with absolute control. There's nothing in Western society like those two absolutes. But that's what acting is – absolute freedom with absolute control. That paradox produces something else – the performance.'

That control is always there, particularly in the most demanding, most emotional scenes. Bernhardt was once asked what she thought about while playing a particularly dramatic scene and she said what – or perhaps it was who – she was going to have for her supper. Glenda does think about matters not connected with the emotional storm through which she is navigating the character she is playing, but it is never something external to the performance itself. It is more on the lines of, 'Was that a cough?' 'Is this too slow?' 'Did they hear that?'

'There's part of you that is always in control and there's part of you that never is. That's what keeps it alive so that you sometimes surprise yourself. The thing about acting is that the parameters are defined – you've got to be heard and you've got to be understood, and what you do has to be seen. They are the absolutes. Within them you can do pretty well what you like as long as it's true to the character and the play. But if you lose yourself in an emotion you lose the audience too.'

Does she never weep, really weep for Hecuba?

'Oh yes, I weep all right. In rehearsal. It's often happened to me. You go through all that. That's when you find the other things. I can cry real tears every night when it's necessary. I mean it's real water that comes out of my eyes, but I'm not really crying. If you really cry you can't speak properly.

'The acting is the same whether it's for the stage or the camera, but the externals are different. In films you do tiny pieces and can sit there all day waiting to do a bit. You've got plenty of time to think about it. On film you have to make every second full of life; it has to be charged with something. It doesn't really matter what as long as it's alive.'

She enlarged on this aspect of acting in an interview with Gordon Gow for *Films and Filming** 'A play – if it's a good play – is constructed in such a way as to feed the actors as much as the audience. You get nourishment from its construction and from its incident, and from where things are placed in relation to one another. And you have an intrinsic pacing within a play. It's not an accident that a play lasts two hours or two-and-a-half hours or whatever; its length is the actual emotional time it can carry. But you don't have that with a film because there you have mainly takes which are thirty or forty-five or sixty seconds long. For each of those takes the emotional content is total. Yet there is nothing that feeds you – because often you have a three hour wait while the set-up and the lighting are changed before you have to make the next emotional commitment.'

When she was making *The Incredible Sarah* in which she played Sarah Bernhardt, she had a great problem with Bernhardt's easy pronouncements on the nature of acting. 'I found I couldn't say the words,' she told Gow, 'my throat choked. And I said, "I can't say this because acting is not this definable!" . . . from what Bernhardt said and from what people wrote down about her you could have asked her what acting in the theatre was and she would have a different, deeply-felt belief for every day in the week.'

---

* January, 1978.

On the following pages:

Four of Elizabeth's six faces:
a) as the princess.
b) as the Queen in episode four, *Horrible Conspiracies*.
c) in episode five, *The Enterprise of England*.
d) Elizabeth the old in the final episode, *Sweet England*.

51

Never a Rainy Tuesday

Glenda's first Oscar came with *Women in Love*, Larry Kramer's screenplay of the D.H. Lawrence novel in which she appeared with Jennie Linden, Alan Bates and Oliver Reed. Ken Russell directed.

Glenda confessionally declares: 'I have to say I am not a Lawrence fan. I like his early stuff when he was writing directly out of his own environment, but I don't have a lot of time for his basic philosophy about the male/female struggle. But Gudrun was a marvellous part because she's genuinely mysterious. At least she's aware of the mysteries possible in life and however phoney she is – and I think she's a very pseud character in many ways – she does have a capacity to inquire and to be surprised. So it was very interesting to do.'

Once again, it was a woman writer, Penelope Mortimer, doing a guest stint on *The Observer* who responded very positively to the performance. 'Every movement expresses the passionate longing of a frigid woman for freedom and domination,' she wrote,★ 'The difficult, uncompromising face, becomes beautiful; she flings herself about in a kind of trapped ecstasy and withdraws into inaccessible contempt. Nothing she does is facile or unconsidered.'

'I like Russell,' says Glenda. 'He's got all those warts and bumps, but I like him as a person and as a director he's like all really good directors – he leaves you alone. Bad directors tell you what they want; good directors always wait to be surprised. The really good ones, more instinctively than deliberately, create an atmosphere, a climate, in which you work well, that helps you produce ideas. That's the thing I like about him most. He doesn't know anything about acting. He'll

---

★ November 16, 1969.

spend hours getting the set right or screaming abuse at people because a costume isn't absolutely correct in every fine detail, and then he'll leave you to play a scene entirely on your own. He can't do anything to help the bad actor.'

Russell himself once said*: 'Working with Glenda has been a very great experience simply because I don't have to say anything whatsoever to her.' He recalled their first meeting: 'When she walked into the room I found myself watching her varicose veins more than her face and only later, when I saw her in the movie of *Marat/Sade* did I realise what a magnificent screen personality she was. I couldn't quite understand it. Sometimes she looked plain ugly, sometimes just plain and then sometimes the most beautiful creature one had ever seen. For the role of Charlotte Corday in *Marat/Sade* she'd worn a long dress and the veins were not in evidence. But our film, *Women in Love*, was set in the 'twenties with plenty of ankle and a good deal more. Glenda is not one to let a few veins stand between her and stardom and so out they came.'

Her next film with Russell was *The Music Lovers* with a screenplay by Melvyn Bragg based on a book by C.D. Bowen, based on the unsatisfactory marriage between Tchaikovsky and Antonina Ivanovna Millukov (whom he left less than a month after the wedding, though it seemed longer in the film). It was a union described by Gerald Abrahams in his biography of Tchaikovsky as 'a marriage of a homosexual to a nymphomaniac,' a situation of which Russell took spectacular advantage. Izvestia called Russell a 'hard-line anti-Communist priest of pornography', though it does not follow from that that it was a particularly good film.

Possibly the most spectacular sequence involved Glenda writhing naked on the floor of a railway compartment while the soundtrack blasted out Shostakovich's 'The Execution of Stepan Razin'. In shooting the sequence, Russell surrounded the set with 12-inch louspeakers and thought, 'Here's this lady

---

* Quoted by Marowitz in his *N.Y. Times* magazine article.

from the Royal Shakespeare Company lying naked like a piece of meat on the floor being bombarded with this music. I wonder if it's distracting her from what she thinks she should be doing in this scene. So I said, "Glenda, I know you don't usually work like this. In the RSC I know it's all hours of intellectual chat with Peter Brook. Would you prefer to do the scene without the music." Like lightning she said, "Christ, if you stopped the music I couldn't do it." Which was fine because I'd made up my mind I was going to use it anyway, whatever her answer, so I just played it louder than ever.'

'Acting,' said Glenda, 'always puts you in a life and death situation. But in that particular film everybody was living at the extremes of their lives. No one had a rainy Tuesday in that movie.'

'Glenda Jackson,' says Michael Billington in his book, *The Modern Actor*, * '. . . speaking subjectively . . . lacks sensuality and sex appeal: what she has in its stead is a glittering irony and steely masculine drive. She is also completely free from that cursed English vice of genteel and ladylike restraint. In Ken Russell's *The Music Lovers* she triumphantly brought off a scene in which, as Tchaikovsky's wife, she was obliged in the course of a violent quarrel to claw the carpet; along with the noise of arrows being released from their bows in Olivier's *Henry V*, the grating of her finger nails against the cloth is one of the ineradicable sounds of modern cinema.'

'That arose by chance out of rehearsal,' Glenda told Gordon Gow in the *Films and Filming* interview. 'I suddenly did it and thought what marvellous noise it was for the expression of that emotion. And we kept it in.'

Describing Russell's methods, she says: 'I had a close-up in another of Nina's fantasy sequences and I'm standing there, done up to the nines, and all I have to do is to walk into the room where I see Tchaikovsky. All I'm actually looking at is a mark on a camera. I walk in and look at this mark and it goes on and on – this for a 10-second close-up. And it went

---

* Hamish Hamilton, 1973

on and on and I thought, "Jesus Christ, the film's going to run out." Eventually, I broke the great rule and said, "Aren't you ever going to say cut?" Later I was going on to Chris Gable about this and I said, "That fucker, he does it deliberately. He just likes to make you sweat." He said, "It isn't that at all. He just waits to see what you're going to do next. The longer he watches and wait, the more you do. And he just watches and waits, watches and waits." '

She has recalled the actual shooting of the railway carriage scene.** 'They started rocking the coach to simulate the movement of the train. First a champagne bucket, glasses, a chicken and knives and forks fell on me and I'm covered with broken glass and superficial cuts and Ken is there shouting, "Wipe the blood off her, clean her up; it will never show."

'Then heavy luggage fell on me and Russell said, "Never mind, get on with it, the bruising doesn't show." Then the cameraman falls right into my lap and he says, "OK, it's all right. I'm a married man." '

She has only worked one day with Russell since *The Music Lovers* and he kept her in a plaster cast for twelve hours. 'It was my punishment for refusing to do *The Devils* she says. Russell had wanted her for *The Devils* and, according to Marowitz, she had agreed to play Sister Jeanne, an abbess so obsessed by the lascivious reputation of the priest, Grandier, that she claims to be possessed by him. Russell described a scene in which, after her death, Sister Jeanne's head is cut off, placed in a glass casket and installed on the convent altar, there to become an object of homage with nuns going on their knees to it.

But the scene was cut and when Glenda was sent the final script, she said, according the Russell, according to Marowitz, 'That's not the way you told it to me.'

'I had to admit that was true,' said Russell. 'She had loved the idea of her head in a casket and everyone worshipping her on their knees. With all that gone she'd have just been back

---

** Interview with Joe Steeples, Daily Mail, September 19, 1981

in the madhouse again.'

Glenda says: 'When I said no to *The Devils* it produced the most bilious fury from him, so there was an exchange of heated letters and I didn't hear from him for ages. Then he rang up and asked me to do a day for him on *The Boy Friend*. So I did.'

Russell's way with Sandy Wilson's pastiche musical of the twenties was to set it as a Busby Berkeley backstage drama in which the leading lady of a tatty touring company breaks her leg and the kid from the chorus, played by Twiggy, gets her big chance. It was *42nd Street* all over again – barring the fact that it was Portsmouth, not Broadway – with Glenda in the Bebe Daniels role and a plaster cast.

That same year Glenda made *Sunday Bloody Sunday* with Peter Finch, directed by John Schlesinger. Finch played a homosexual Jewish doctor uneasy with his sexual orientation and uncomfortable with his ancestry. Glenda was a business-woman sharing her young lover (Murray Head) with him. Something happened on that film – which won Finch an Oscar nomination and Glenda the best actress award from the British Film Academy – which, for her, precisely illustrated the peculiar demands made by the camera. She told Gordon Gow: 'A separate crew from BBC-TV was there doing a film about the making of our film. Well, obviously they couldn't shoot a TV take while we were actually performing for the film itself. So, in one instance when we had done a rather long take three or four times, John Schlesinger said, 'Okay. That's fine for me. Now would you mind doing it again for television? Well we did it immediately. There was no wait. There was nothing you could lose – or so you would think. And yet when I did it for the television film camera it was not at all the same sort of performance I'd given for the cinema camera. And that is because the minute the film director says to you, "Okay, we've got that," it's expunged from your mind. You drop. You stop. There's nothing left over. So what I did for television was just a repetitious thing which didn't have the same edge to it – although if John had said he wanted to go on to as many as fourteen takes for the film itself we would still have been able to perform as we had originally because it would still be the

56

With Walter Matthau in *Hopscotch*, the second of the two films they made together.

specific film we were making.'

She dislikes television, though her major impact on the general public, not only in Britain but overseas, was made through the television series, *Elizabeth R* in which, in the course of six episodes, she aged from 16 to 69.

She enjoyed playing Elizabeth but finds television a boring medium. 'Mind you,' she says, 'now that they make most television plays as films it's really like making a film. But to work to a television camera is pointless. It's not interested in what you're doing; it's just as happy photographing its fellow cameras.'

But surely, a camera is camera, whether it's a television or a film camera?

'No it isn't. A film camera is rooted to you. Television cameras are always being moved around. To do a play in a television studio is to have the worst of both mediums. You still shoot out of context like in a film, but you shoot half an hour of playing time in one go, something that never happens on film. Also I don't like being part of 24 hours of entertainment. There's no sense of occasion. Television doesn't make the right kind of demands on you; it just doesn't.'

Not even the Morecambe and Wise show?

'Oh no, that was the best.'

But some people were critical – great actress lowering herself by appearing with clowns, that sort of thing.

'Silly sods. Peak of my career, Morecambe and Wise. It was where the fantasies came true. Fred and Ginge. It's all been downhill since then.'

Despite her general feelings about television, she acknowledges that playing Elizabeth was a wonderful opportunity and an important step in her career. 'To play that age development without it becoming an acting trick, without someone saying, "cor, look at 'er, she's playing 69 and she's only – whatever." That in itself was extraordinary and it was also extraordinary to work for over seven months with the same group of people because characters recurred all the time. The individual scripts varied in quality. Some were very good, some were just all right and some were awful. The best was the one about the Armada.

'But it was a very interesting series to do as it ran on both the personal and the state level. Women with power, feminism – none of those things were relevant to her or to her time. Most of the decisions she made, particularly at the beginning of her life, were simply to stay alive. She had to be extremely clever otherwise she would have been killed. And when she was actually ruling, the interesting thing is how little power she actually wielded, how little power any ruler actually wields. She would never make a decision, just hope that time would alter circumstances. The checks and balances of the time were far more due to the personalities than to the structure of the state. Fear was a very potent check and conflicting ambitions created a balance of power.

'The most difficult thing for me always was the reality of believing that God had chosen you. She had an absolute certainty about it; I found it very hard to bring it into play. The whole element of religion which at that time veered between black and white magic, that whole mystic thing, I found very difficult to use imaginatively and relate it to anything I could recognise.

'I think I understand people who have opted for a religious life, though I don't know whether it's the religion or simply that I admire that kind of discipline. But I find it very difficult to understand religion as the tangible force it was then. That whole area of necromancy and alchemy and fate and all that was difficult for me to use because I couldn't rationalise it for myself.'

Elizabeth R was sold to 64 countries and won her two Emmies in America, one for the best dramatic actress in a series and the other for the best single performance – as the dying Elizabeth in the final episode.

Among its admirers in America was the actor George Segal who, some years before, had seen Glenda in the *Marat/ Sade* in New York and had walked out of it because he found it too horrifying.

'When I saw Glenda in the *Elizabeth R* series,' says Segal, 'I thought "here is a consummate actress." I had never really heard of her. *Women in Love* and *The Music Lovers* were rather obscure to me – foreign movies as far as I was concerned. But in the Elizabeth series she played every card in the deck and when you talk to her about it, all she wants to discuss is the four hours of agonising make-up every morning as the old Elizabeth.

'But when I think of the Elizabeth series, I think of her when she was young, with long red hair and filled with fire. And I was dazzled by it because she was *acting* and I understand what the process is.'

Melvin Frank, who directed and (with Jack Rose) wrote *A Touch of Class*, had taken a dip in his career, says Segal. 'His last big successes had been the Bob Hope pictures and this, to him, was a remake of a Bob Hope-Lucille Ball film.* Originally, the money people wanted Sophia Loren and Dustin Hoffman for *A Touch of Class* but Mel had seen me in *The Owl and the Pussycat* with Barbra Streisand and he wanted us. Then he saw a Morecambe and Wise Christmas show on television and saw Glenda dance – as Ginger Rogers, I think to their Fred Astaire – and he wanted Glenda for the role. And me.

'When I first saw Glenda she was in a t-shirt and blue jeans and I wondered how she was ever going to play a glamorous dress designer. Then on the first day she walked on for a photography session and she took my breath away. When we started to make the film she astonished me by the love, the compassion, the depth and subtlety of her acting. She would give you a line perfectly logically but always with a flip at the end, always with a twist. I was acting like I had never acted before. I am a performer; she's an actress and I think that's why it was such a great combination. I'd been brought up in cabaret theatre, improvisational theatre; she had her performance when she arrived on the set; I had no idea what I was going to do **.

---

* Probably *The Facts of Life*, 1960, written by Mel Frank and Norman Panama in which a couple of married suburbanites have an abortive love affair.
** He did not seem to know about the Theatre of Cruelty.

'We were instant brother and sister and Mel was our father. It had the kind of intimacy that went way beyond a lover relationship. The film wasn't a sex farce, though it was sexy. Mel said the whole thing probably turned at that moment when her legs went up in the air and suddenly it became sexy. You've gotta have that in movies. On the stage it's not necessary; there's a kind of sexual vitality. But *A Touch of Class* was an enormously sexual film which is why it still lives.'

The picture follows the course of a hectic affair between a London dress designer and an American on a business trip to Europe. The depth of feeling, mainly created by the depth of the performances, gives it a rare quality. The pleasure and the pain of love are mirrored and seediness is kept at bay. Some people hated it. Sheridan Morley in *The Times* thought it was a disastrous example of what happens if you shoot for high comedy and miss; but Derek Malcolm in *The Guardian* said: 'We laugh at the sheer folly which these two supremely egotistical people embark on their adventure, pursue it and then end it.'

Says Segal: 'Mel was smart enough to tell us not to play the comedy but to play it for real and we both had a background of playing reality. My timing ain't bad either. But it was a new step for both of us. We met on the playground, raw and unschooled, both from different backgrounds, and it all came together. That's what they call chemistry.'

Segal was well aware that he was being paired with a powerful actress. One of his impressions from the Elizabeth series was that Glenda had overwhelmed the actors who had appeared with her.

'All those guys – Robert Hardy, Daniel Massey – were all eaten alive,' Segal says. 'There was carnage, nobody left after she'd finished with them.'

He put his trust in the training imposed by the American star system where 'you have to step up to whoever you are with or get ploughed under. There's a kind of gambler's energy – Matthau's got it more than anyone else – a racetrack, ballsy kind of Las Vegas energy, that is able to deal with the stuff that actresses like Glenda and Streisand put out, that Queen Elizabeth, Queen Victoria stuff. Powerhouses. It's Maggie

Hedda Gabler,
with Jennie Linden as Mrs Elvsted.

Thatcher. Glenda's got to have good feelings about her. She's gotta be delighted that there's somebody like that around. She may hate her as a politician, but it's somebody she can match, toe to toe. At the same time there's something very moving about Glenda, something touching.'

The offscreen relationship is complex and liable to misinterpretation. When, some five years later, Mel Frank tried to repeat the success of *A Touch of Class* and matched Segal and Glenda together again in *Lost and Found* a visitor to the Toronto studio where it was shot was firmly convinced that they would not be seen dead together once out of sight of the camera.*

'That's a little exaggerated,' says Segal. 'We'd meet before the scene when we were both in character, exchange some small talk in character and play the scene. Once it was over we'd walk away, she to her place, me to mine. She always has a little group of people around her, hairdresser, make-up, wardrobe, people like that, people she can put her feet up with, have a cigarette and relax. We didn't walk away because we disliked each other but because the scene was over.

'The first car ride we ever took together alone, the driver in front, the two of us in the back, she whistled for most of the journey. The first time I made any real contact with her was over Paul Scofield. He's God to her. So I became acrimonious about him, found fault, criticised. We insulted each other – at least we insulted each other's opinions. She loves it. That's the relationship she has with her sisters and with certain other people. She can be very acid with people, really cut them, but if you cut back you're suddenly in a duel and it starts to get fun. And that's brothers and sisters; they're the only ones who have the right to criticise each other.

'But after you've played a scene you walk away because it's over and when the film is over there's a great emptiness because part of acting is giving something of yourself to the person you're acting with, even if it's only in terms of the

---

* Anthea Disney report, Daily Mail, June 6, 1978

character you are playing. And what you give they take away with them.'

Lost and Found was not a great success. 'It was made for a price,' says Segal, 'and everybody got out okay. It just lost energy.'

While in London he went to see her in her current play and called backstage afterwards. A few weeks later Glenda was a guest at his wedding at Westminster Synagogue.

'There are lots of people I've worked with,' says Glenda, 'and in a rehearsal room I'll talk a million to the dozen. But I have absolutely nothing to say to them when we're not working together. That isn't the case with George. While we were doing *Lost and Found* I think he was going through a pretty bad time himself. I think we are friends, but there really is no necessity for friendship in a work situation. It's often the case with actors. You have close relationships with them and then you never see them for years and it doesn't make any difference, you are still friends. There are, of course, other actors you loath.'

She has had no personal experience of a close on-screen relationship continuing off-screen. 'When that kind of thing happens,' she says, 'it has nothing to do with the fact that they are acting – other than propinquity, of course. Working with someone can be very intimate because there is no time for the usual social exchanges. On *Sunday Bloody Sunday* I met Tony Britton for the first time in my life. Schlesinger introduced us one morning at 8 o'clock and we shook hands. "Right," said Schlesinger, "Take off your clothes and get into bed." And that was it. Ludicrous! Crazy!'

Sunday Bloody Sunday with Peter Finch was a triumph; the next film she made with him was disastrous. She was cast as Emma Hamilton in Terence Rattigan's *Bequest to the Nation* with Finch playing Nelson. Finch knew that his heart was giving out and the director, James Cellan Jones, would have preferred someone who looked physically more like the buxom Emma – Ava Gardner or Elizabeth Taylor were his preferences, he told Trader Faulkner for his biography of Peter Finch.* But producer Hal Wallis insisted on Glenda for the role and he, of course, had his way.

Faulkner quotes Jones: 'Emma Hamilton was 14½ stones, Glenda is about seven, but Hal Wallis's choice was final. What went wrong with the picture to my mind was that Glenda, who is a really fine actress, was woefully miscast and she knew it. She is too good an actress not to know it went sour on her.'

What is more, Glenda pre-empted the critics and announced that her performance was rotten even before the press showing of the film. Writing in *The Guardian*, a baffled Derek Malcolm said: 'It comes to something when the leading lady of a big commercial feature allows herself to be quoted on the Women's Page of *The Guardian* as saying she gave a lousy performance, later compounding the folly even more vehemently on the telly.' He was further puzzled, he added, because he couldn't agree with her. Others did. Cecil Wilson in the *Daily Mail* said that he could not vouch for Lady Hamilton's behaviour in public but found it hard to believe that she had disgraced Nelson 'as monstrously as Glenda Jackson disgraces Peter Finch in this picture.'

And he went on to say that the 'sleazy, boozy, belching, foul-mouthed trollop presented in Terence Rattigan's adaptation of his stage play seems to me more Glenda (screen Glenda that is) than Emma.'*

Faulkner says that there had been great tension on the set between Finch and Glenda and that Finch was furious when she had announced that it was a bad picture. So was Rattigan who is reported to have remarked that she had not offered to return her fee.

'I should never have done it,' says Glenda. 'I don't like Rattigan's stuff and I don't know how to play it. Also I loathed the director. Instead of doing what I should have done which was to scream and rage and behave like a spoilt Hollywood star, I behaved very well. When I was asked about the film I had to tell the truth and the truth was that I was fucking terrible in it. It's not a good film anyway.'

---

* Angus and Robertson, 1979.

* It is difficult to recognise any of Glenda's screen roles in that description.

But Glenda has not behaved like a Hollywood star, even in Hollywood. Her first American film was in 1977 when she made *House Calls* with Walter Matthau and there were those who immediately started to talk about them as the new Tracy-Hepburn team. This was to misread Glenda entirely, for though she was to make another film with Matthau, it is impossible to see her making any long-term commitment to any particular genre, least of all romantic comedy.

She adjusted quickly to American studio behaviour and, it seems, they soon got used to her which must have been far more difficult. She was, after all, the first actress in film history to set foot in Hollywood for the first time already in possession of two Oscars. Nor did she make any secret of the fact that, pleased as she was to have them, they were doing service on her mother's sideboard as bookends.

'It's true,' she says, 'that on the first day I arrived at the studio I thought I was going to be stifled by the respect that was being exuded from every pore but after I'd effed and blinded a couple of times they stopped being quite so respectful and we got down to the business of actually working.

'The thing about Hollywood is that you get respect only so long as you can deliver. No quarter's given or expected. So the over-riding pressures stay pretty much the same. The external pressures on people who are stars within the American system are horrendous, but the interesting thing is that the real pressures are on those people who are stars on television, not film.

'I worked with Carole Burnett and Jim Garner in a film (*Health*, directed by Robert Altman). Carole had had a hugely successful series that ran for eleven years and Jim was just coming to the end of *The Rockford Files*. We were in Florida and there was something like a scene from *Suddenly Last Summer* (in which a homosexual poet is raped and murdered by beach boys). I saw Jim run the length of a beach pursued by hundreds of women. Really all they wanted to do was to say, "We think you're great". Carole had to move hotels four times because people would knock her up in the middle of the night for an autograph.* Neither of them could go to a

66

restaurant or shop. It's the pattern of their lives if they move out of Los Angeles. In Los Angeles nobody bothers them. I've never experienced this kind of pressure because I've never done a long-running series on television. Television denies the mystique; people think they own you. There's no barrier.

'The great cinema stars always played the same person and they had whole industries, galaxies of people to support them and make it possible. I don't have anything to sell in that area and, besides, it's not the age for that kind of thing. All I am is an actress. When I say that's *all* I am it sounds pejorative and I don't mean it that way. I take acting very seriously, but I don't necessarily take myself seriously when I'm not doing it. I'm not a guaranteed surefire success because I don't do stuff that is always very popular. I'd sooner not work than do work I don't like and that, I suppose, is very egotistical. In fact I'd sooner do a play that nobody but me liked than do one that everyone liked and I didn't.'

Even when offered a great deal of money?

'Ah, people only ever offer you a great deal of money for rubbish. The greater the number of noughts on the cheque, the greater the crapular content of the movie; the better the work, the less you're paid.'

Her agent, Peter Crouch, says that an American producer wanted her for a re-make of *The Maltese Falcon* in which she would play the role originally taken by Mary Astor. Glenda read the script and decided that the character was one-dimensional, cardboard. 'She's all enigma,' she said. 'All she does is to stare and look' so she turned it down.

The American asked to speak to Glenda personally and said: 'I'm told you won't do this for a million dollars.'

'That's an obscene sum of money to offer anybody,' she said. 'And I'm still not doing it.'

Says Crouch: 'He sent her a bunch of orchids so big they could hardly get it through the door. With it was a card saying, "With great respect." '

---

* American readers should adjust that sentence to read: '. . . people would wake her up in the middle of the night . . .'

'In America,' says Glenda, 'the money is part of the pecking order. It actually does make a difference to your way of life if you are only a half a million star instead of a million. It's an insane place. But I enjoy working with Americans. They work very directly. A lot of English acting is surreptitious. There are actors in England who are capable of being concerned and committed and who regard the day's work they are doing as the most important of their life. But there are others who believe that you're supposed to pretend you're doing it between *The Times* crossword or something really important like the cricket score. I find all that very hard to take. The Americans are never amateurs. They throw it at you directly and you have to be able to throw it back. I like that very much.

'It's the prevailing attitude in this country that it doesn't really matter – or at least they have to *pretend* that it doesn't really matter. Obviously there's a life outside acting, but when you're doing it there's nothing else.'

There has been comedy on film but very little on stage.

'An accident,' she says. 'It's just what you're offered. Good comedies are few and far between and, anyway, we're not in a comic age. Comedy is either funny peculiar at an extreme level (she expressed distaste) or it is revivals of Nöel Coward.'

There was a helpless shrug signalling more distaste. No Amanda she. Even when she is not acting, she is open, accessible, her feelings signalled clearly and unmistakeably. It is almost as if she had fewer – perhaps none – of the veils with which most people cover any display of naked feeling.

'There's more comedy in the cinema,' she says, 'and it's much harder to do than drama. It's not true that laugh and the world laughs with you. It's very hard to make a group of people laugh at the same thing; much easier to make them cry at the same thing. If you don't time it right you don't get the laugh but if you time it right and the life's not there you still don't get the laugh. Being able to balance the two all the time is very difficult. That's why great comic acting is probably the greatest acting there is.'

She not only projects strong feeling, she arouses it. Few

As Stevie Smith,
the North London poet.

people are indifferent to her. When she was playing Lotte in the Botho Strauss play, *Great and Small* in London* one man walked out at the interval and asked for his money back. Not content with that, he demanded to see the company manager and told him: 'How can this woman who played Elizabeth the First allow herself to say these terrible words?'

'Up till then,' says Glenda, 'the only four-letter word I had used had been "shit." But it's happened before. I think people want their opinions confirmed and often confuse the part with the performer.'

On the provincial tour that preceded London, the play, which in its original version runs for more than five hours but had been cut to about two and a quarter, had caused audiences some distress because, it was said, many people could not understand it and had indicated their disapproval by leaving noisily. It must have been an arduous tour.

'Arduous? That's irrelevant. I've not felt that it was arduous,' Glenda says as we talk in her dressing room between matinée and evening performance. 'When you're working you don't have that sort of exhaustion because you've always got to be digging away at something. We've never stopped rehearsing and by Saturday night I'm tired, but it's not the complete sort of wipe-out you might think because I haven't found it all. And it's so short a run I won't have found it all by the time we're finished. That's the great value of doing a play like this – it always makes demands on you and you never have to create an interest or find a way of raising your energy levels. It's just there, waiting like a bloody great mountain and you have to climb it. Sometimes you do and sometimes you don't.'

And when you don't is it because there are times when you don't feel physically up to it? A headache, perhaps?

'The lousy performance never has anything to do with externals. That's one of the great irritants of acting – that you cannot programme yourself always for excellence. If it had anything to do with the way you feel, you should give your

---

* Vaudeville Theatre, from August 25-October 15, a planned limited run.

worse performances when you're not feeling well and you're best when you are. But it usually works the other way around. That's what's so bloody irritating. It's not a tap you can just turn on.'

Perhaps private emotions sometimes interfere with a performance?

'How do you mean, private?'

'Such as when your marriage broke up after 17 years. There must have been a fraught period.'

'I still went on and did whatever it was that I was doing. I can't remember. But I would hope it wouldn't make a difference. In fact I think it's the other way around actually. I think work can often impinge on private life.

'Why some performances should be better than others is a continuing mystery.* Obviously, audiences have a lot to do with it. The more an audience gives you back, the more you can give them. But it's not always that. There have been wonderful performances given in front of lousy audiences. You can't do theatre without an audience but most audiences want what they've liked before. Certainly in London, though it's better than it was because the foreign tourist stays later and later. To actually get an audience that comes in and sits down and waits to see what's going to happen and opens its eyes and ears to what you're doing is very rare. You meet it more outside London and you meet it even more outside England.

'You have to tell audiences what to think. You have to make them go the way the playwright wants them to go. And that's a difficult process. Sometimes if you're with the Royal Shakespeare Company and it's one of those club performances you spend all your time beating them off the stage, they're so anxious to be up there with you. You're almost kicking them back into their seats. Other nights you've got to go out and drag them out of their seats and shake them into some kind of awareness.

* Aha!

'An audience can be ferocious. They can tear you limb from limb. They are the enemy in a sense because they'd just as soon not listen to what you are saying, not understand what the writer is writing about, not be bothered. I don't like audiences. I don't think acting is a popularity contest. The easiest thing in the world is to go out there – and this is the besetting sin of English acting – and make an audience like you. You just let them see how *hard* it is to act.

'Some people,' she says, 'have built their careers on it. Olivier's one. Olivier always shows you what a marvellous actor he is by showing you how difficult it is. And I despise that. I despise the attitude and I despise the people who like it. That isn't what acting is about.

'Really, all you do as an actress is to be a funnel or pipe, a means of transmitting a writer to the audience. That's all you are.'

This is nonsense, as any writer would testify who has ever had a line of dialogue invested with a deeper significance or a funnier meaning than he had thought was possible, when he wrote it.

'All the same,' says Glenda, 'the demands of the play are pre-eminent and if you distort it by giving less than you are capable of giving how do you look at yourself in the mirror when you come to take your make-up off?'

Some Crackers

When Michael Billington published his book, *The Modern Actor* in 1973 it appeared to him that Glenda Jackson had been more or less lost to the stage. He recalled the moment in *Mary, Queen of Scots* – in which she played Elizabeth to Vanessa Redgrave's Mary – when she delivered a blow to the Earl of Dudley's solar plexus that, Billington said, would have felled Mohammed Ali. 'Here I felt,' he added, 'was the Lady Macbeth of her generation if only she had not virtually foresworn stage acting in favour of the movies.'

In the decade that followed Glenda made 14 films, three of them – *The Maids, Hedda Gabler* and *Stevie* being based on stage productions in which she had recently appeared. There were five other plays in the same period, among them *Antony and Cleopatra* for the Royal Shakespeare Company.

It seems quite incredible that she should complain – as indeed she frequently does – of being under-used.

'She's a workaholic,' says Susannah York who appeared with her in *The Maids* at the Greenwich Theatre and in the subsequent movie.

Genet's *The Maids* has been described as a hall of mirrors, a black mass, an erotic ritual, a fantasy of servility and revolt and, an idealisation of murder as a means of self-expression and status. It concerns two maids, sisters, Claire and Solange who, whenever their mistress is out, take turns to enact a fantasy of servility and authority in which one plays the mistress and the other the maid. They have engineered the arrest of their lady's lover, referred to only as 'Monsieur', by writing anonymous letters and then they discover he is out on bail. Terrified of being found out, they decide to kill their mistress when she returns by poisoning her tea. They do not tell her of Monsieur's release but, as she is about to drink the tea, she finds out and hurries off to meet him. The maids resume their game. Claire plays the lady and demands the poisoned cup of tea. She drinks it and dies.

There are numerous possible interpretations and Genet, ideally, wanted men to play all the roles. At the Greenwich Theatre in February 1974, they were played by Glenda Jackson and Susannah York as the maids and Vivien Merchant as the mistress. It might perhaps have worked better if Susannah York had exchanged places with Vivien Merchant, for the mistress is said to be younger and more beautiful than the maids (and sexual jealousy is a potent force in the play) and that, sadly, can be said more easily now that Vivien Merchant, formerly the wife of Harold Pinter, is dead. But it is an unrewarding role with the character more off than on and it is not easy to see either Susannah York or Glenda Jackson accepting it.

'I had looked forward to working with Glenda,' says Susannah York. 'She has a lot of the qualities I like and I think I have some of them myself. Though we are very unalike in many respects, we both, I think, have a fierce dedication to our work. I love people who work hard and she works wonderfully hard, so it's incredibly stimulating.

'But Glenda doesn't pull her punches and we had our share of arguments. I think in our different ways we're both very forceful, very strong. If I hold to a conviction I hold to it, unless somebody comes up with something better. So we had quite a lot of arguments and disagreements. It wasn't by any means plain sailing and we had a few verbal battles about points of characterisation or what was the aim of a scene. Sometimes she might feel I wasn't helping her enough in what she saw as her goal; and I might feel the same with her.

'On the other hand we had a very healthy respect for each other's talents and personality – at least I had for her's. Trying to look at it objectively – and she might not agree with this – I would tend to think that perhaps tact is slightly more natural to me than it is to her. I set a lot of score by tactfulness if I think I can get my own way by it. I always feel it is better to hold one's big guns for the big battle. I'm always aware that there may be a big battle on all projects and productions and that something will eventually come up that I simply cannot budge on. So that if there's any way for me to include another point of view and achieve the same result I'm prepared, for

In a blonde wig, as Eva Braun, with Georgina Hale as Clara Petacci in *Summit Conference*. *Photo*: Donald Cooper.

the sake of harmony, to see if there's a way I can go round it. But I am quite as obstinate as Glenda and if I cannot adjust or accommodate, then it's a battle out in the open.

'Glenda knows that actors work in different ways and she held herself back to see what would happen. I suppose we circled around each other for a while at the beginning, but I think we were supported by this tremendous respect and actual affection – certainly on my part – for I really *liked* Glenda, I like her enormously. And I never like anyone if I cannot respect them. I actually felt a warm, sisterly affection for her. But I quarrel with my sisters and Glenda and I were also playing sisters and that rather conditioned our feelings towards each other. It was a good sisterly relationship – with the frankness that goes with it. I came out of it feeling a tremendous warmth for her.

'As far as Vivien was concerned, we were aware that we had to handle her with kid gloves. Glenda and I knew that when the chips were down we could be straight and honest with each other. Vivien was a slightly different generation, a very different personality.

'I'd welcome a chance of working with Glenda again. I love working with terrific actors; it brings something extra out of me. I thought Glenda was better in the film than in the theatre, absolutely wonderful. That driving energy was there all the time, every day, take after take.'

American producer Robert Enders filmed *The Maids* for about 250,000 dollars, the three actresses working for modest fees but on a percentage of the profit. Then along came another American producer, Ely Landau who, in a co-venture with American Express, had made a number of films of such important stage productions as Simon Gray's *Butley*, Harold Pinter's *The Homecoming*, John Osborne's *Luther*, and Brecht's *Galileo* for what was called the American Film Theatre. They needed an additional film to make up some magic number and bought *The Maids* for half a million dollars, the three actresses thus getting substantial sums before the film was even shown.

One of the by-products of the film was that Enders and Glenda formed Bowden Productions which went on to make *Nasty Habits*, *Hedda Gabler* and *Stevie*.

Says Enders: 'Many people thought *The Maids* was the best of all the American Film Theatre programme; Glenda got another Academy nomination for *Hedda* and *Stevie* won virtually every critics' award going, but wasn't eligible for the Academy Awards because of some cock-up in the distribution.'

It was ineligible because it had been shown for two weeks in Los Angeles the year before it opened in New York and attracted serious attention. The Academy Awards can apply only to those films shown for the first time in the USA in the year of the awards. When it reached New York, Vincent Carby wrote an enthusiastic review of *Stevie* for *The New York Times* and the result, says Hugh Whitemore who wrote the play, was '*Stevie* mania.'

He had, in fact, written the play about eight years before it was staged in London in 1977. It was based on the externally uneventful life of the poet, Stevie Smith, an unmarried lady who lived with her aunt in a small Victorian terrace in the North London suburb of Palmer's Green and was on intimate terms with quiet desperation and death, both of which she faced with an unflinching acceptance of their place in her life. She died in 1969.

'Everybody turned it down,' says Whitemore, 'though one well-known actress read it, liked it but didn't want to do it.' It was then sent to Glenda. Whitemore had, in fact, written one of the better scripts in the Elizabeth R television series.

'Glenda,' says Whitemore, 'read it on a Thursday and rang me on Friday to say that she would do it. Then there was a year's wait because of all the other work she was doing. When it was put on Glenda gave a quite astonishing performance.'

'I did *Stevie* because I thought it was impossible,' says Glenda, 'quite impossible to do in the theatre. I thought no audience would sit through a monologue, which is virtually what it is. But the words were wonderful because, apart from a couple of scenes, they are all her words from her novels, poems and letters. It was such a treat to have that quality of language to work on and I found the relationship between her and her aunt marvellous.'

Indeed, the loving respect between Stevie and her aunt,

played on both stage and screen by Mona Washbourne, provided the necessary non-literary balance and resulted in Miss Washbourne getting the London critics' award as the best supporting actress of 1977.

'So,' says Glenda, 'having thought that this was bleedin' impossible, I thought, no it isn't if you just treat the audience as a fourth character. Stevie Smith was a woman who loved to talk so it was a character element as well as being a theatrical device and one could change – not the lines – but one's reactions, depending on how the audience reacted to me.'

The theatre at least has an old-fashioned convention that actors, in certain circumstances, may talk directly to the audience. But the cinema has no such tradition except in broad comedy such as *Hellzapoppin* and the Crosby-Hope films.

'So when it came to the film,' says Glenda, 'I said this isn't going to work, just looking at the camera all the time. So I said if you use the camera as another person – and sometimes you look at a person you are talking to and sometimes you don't – you might be able to get away with it.'

And so they did. Get away with it, that is.

'Glenda,' says Whitemore, who also wrote the screenplay for another of her films, *Return of the Soldier*, 'has got the reputation of being a tough, ballsy actress and her voice is very strong and clear, not a delicate instrument like, say, Dorothy Tutin's. But she has all the qualities of vulnerability and a sort of loneliness. She's a marvellously lonely actress.'

'I liked Stevie Smith,' said Glenda. 'She stood four square and looked the big things straight in the eye.'

The third filmed play of that period, *Hedda Gabler*, was directed by Trevor Nunn in 1975 and staged at the Aldwych Theatre, then the Royal Shakespeare's London home.

This Hedda gave us leave to see her as the useless, cowardly woman she really is instead of the victim of a repressive society which is her own valuation and that, it must be said, of many critics. She was a solitary woman in a society held together by kinship and class. If she had had more brains she would have thought her way out of it; if she had had more courage she would have bolted long ago with Lovborg, the only true creative force in the vicinity whose manuscript she burns in the stove as if she were aborting their unconceived child. Nowhere did Glenda Jackson's performance try to manufacture a claim to intellectual or moral superiority. Her Hedda would be forgotten six months after she shoots herself, not because of the smug shallowness of those who survived her but because she herself would have left nothing behind except self-generated sourness and anger.

Or so it seemed to me at the time.

'We're all indoctrinated about the classic roles,' says Glenda, 'and I'd read Ibsen only in those dreadful Michael Meyer translations. When we came to do this one, Nunn got the text literally translated by a Norwegian friend. It was fascinating to read because Norwegian is a very sparse language and all those people, spoke with individual voices and not like guests at a vicarage tea party. And it was very funny, a mordantly black comedy about Norwegian society.'

Indeed, Max Beerbohm, who hated Hedda, thought that Ibsen meant us to laugh at her and that she should be played by someone with a sense of comedy which Duse, whom he saw in the role, evidently did not possess.

'Hedda isn't a calculating, ruthless woman,' says Glenda. 'She's really rather stupid. They're all big fish in little ponds in the play and I found that fascinating. She has no courage and she's none of the things that she has been told she is. She's always bewailing being stuck in that awful little town, but her husband had taken her all over Europe and she hadn't set Paris on fire and nobody had told her that she was the most remarkable woman they had ever met. All that is very salutary for her and she has to accommodate it somehow when they return. She's tragic if you take tragedy as an inevitable path from which there can be no deviation, but she's certainly no noble tragic figure. They're all second-rate characters with pretentions to being first-rate, Hedda, Tesman, Lovborg. My admiration for Hedda is that she actually acknowledges that there is no way out for her. She could not become any of the things that were expected of her and she chooses not to conform. It's the only element of choice she has. But it's very revealing that she goes behind the curtains to shoot herself. The pressure of respectability is very profound in that play.'

Peter Hall's Diaries, (Hamish Hamilton, 1983) has the following entry:

'Wednesday, 23 July (1975): To *Hedda Gabler* at the Aldwych in the evening. I was riveted by Glenda Jackson. She seems now to have found a way of making her private complexity public without being insistent or indulgent. A great actress in the making. But her performance, though keenly enjoyable, was rather wrong-headed. Hedda should hurl herself at man after man like a moth eagerly going towards a new lamp; she should initially be vital, full of joy. Glenda's Hedda was glum from the word go, bent on a course of self-destruction. I was struck by the fact that this was the last great pre-Freud play. After Freud, nobody could have written so unselfconsciously those scenes between Brack and Hedda about the leading cock in the farmyard, and the importance of a firm, straight pistol when firing . . .'

Says Glenda, with great satisfaction: 'It is always interesting when you play a character that everybody thinks they know and you don't conform to their expectations.'

She was, in fact, speaking before Sir Peter Hall's diaries were published. Had she known of his observations the satisfaction would not have been lessened. The film of *Hedda* has won a large number of awards and, Glenda was pleased to say, was required viewing for students at the Romanian Drama School.

Another destructive lady she was soon to play was Cleopatra to Alan Howard's Antony.

'I must admit,' she said, 'that I have played some crackers in my time.'

It was the first time she had worked with Brook since *US*, except for the abortive Snap, Crackle and Pop *Tempest* ten years earlier in 1968.

One commentator has described Cleopatra as 'a woman of infinite variety but not in the least complex,' and it is an assessment she would not argue with. 'I would read complexity as being psychological complexity where the person actually can't deal with herself. And that's certainly not a problem for Cleopatra. She is an extremely sophisticated savage. She's

Rose. *Photo*: Donald Cooper.

never been disciplined and she's unbridled. That was my view of her and Brook nodded his head to it. He probably changed his mind 30 seconds later. But that's a broad stroke anyway; you can't play it; you have to break it down into detail.

'The overwhelming thing for me, the most difficult thing, was Cleopatra's speed. I mean, she's so fucking *fast*. It's easy enough – well, I mean, it's all right – to play a variety of ever-changing emotions, but to play them so quickly and at the same time to convince the audience that they are experienced at the depth that she feels them – that's difficult. She's not a facile woman and she could actually go from way down to right up in two seconds flat and then around 73 corners – it's the sheer speed of her that I find so astonishing. And on top of that, to find variety in her – I mean, just try finding that infinite variety!

'The life force in her is so strong that it's really very hard for her to bring herself to suicide. There's a parallel link with Antony when he impales himself on his sword.

'I always love working with Brook. But it was very different from the way we had worked before because the last time I'd worked with him in any depth was when we did *US* and we didn't really have any text for weeks. And, before that, in the *Marat/Sade*, we hardly looked at the text for a long time. But with *Cleopatra* we were on that bloody text from the word go. Every morning would be spent in exercises and physical work, but the rest of the time he was always on the text, digging it out.'

Brook surprises by piling one amazing invention on top of another, as in his celebrated 1970 production of *A Midsummer Night's Dream*, or he astonishes by a simplicity so unforced that it actually seems to be a simple matter to bring about. There could be no greater misconception. This *Antony and Cleopatra* fell into the simple category, a clear examination of the text leaving the spectacle to the imagery woven by the words.

Cleopatra, kaftaned and crop-haired, was mercurial, a queen, a woman and, if at all a child, a particularly dangerous one, ruthless in pursuit of the passing passion, greedy for fulfilment not only of physical needs but insatiable for answers, information, news. She was magnificently voiced.

★   ★   ★

Three London productions followed *Antony and Cleopatra* which eventually moved to the Aldwych. In *Rose* by Andrew Davies, at the Duke of York's Theatre (March, 1980) she played a teacher trapped in a marriage from which the magic had fled, saddled with a mother whose idea of enjoying herself was having a bad time and enduring a job in a school run by a headmistress with all the wrong ideas about education. She had a wry, tactless sense of humour and, as played by Glenda, even her flippancy emerged clothed in authority.

In *Summit Conference* at the Lyric (May, 1982) she was Eva Braun, Hitler's mistress, spending an afternoon in a waiting room with Clara Petacci (Georgina Hale), Mussolini's mistress. These two shadows of their masters not unexpectedly cast no illumination on the events in which their originals played so insignificant a role and I see no reason to alter my original feeling that Glenda, having become involved with a script full of commonplace ideas, gave a coarse and confused performance.

In Botho Strauss's *Great and Small* at the Vaudeville (see earlier comments), she was Lotte, a girl so eager to be liked that she was rejected by everyone. These included casual acquaintances, old friends, ex-husband and employer/lover until God forces His presence on her and she finds a kind of smiling happiness walking the streets with a supermarket trolley laden with bulging plastic bags and alarming innocent passers-by with talk of religion.

There were hints that the play was supposed to be an indictment of a society which no longer has room for personal relationships, but it is truly difficult to imagine any kind of society where people like Lotte are accepted. It would be like having to spend all the waking hours trying to please a desperate puppy. A thrilling performance all the same.

In the autumn of 1983, Glenda began work on a film in which she was to play the wife of the Soviet dissident, Andrei Sakharov, a role taken by Jason Robards Junior. Before

Lotte in *Great and Small*, with Barry Stanton.
Photo: Zoe Dominic.

shooting began, Glenda had decided that the dialogue was worthy – not a word of praise in her vocabulary – except where the words were those actually used by the Sakharovs. 'The real always makes the imagined stick out like a sore thumb,' she said. 'So I can see us re-writing it ourselves.'

After the film, directed by Jack Gold, she was, she said, supposed to do a play which would open at the 2,000-seater Ahmanson Theatre in Los Angeles and then, under an exchange agreement arranged by London impresario Duncan Weldon, come to the Theatre Royal, Haymarket. She had wanted to do Brecht's *Mother Courage* but the Royal Shakespeare Company has the rights and, though they have no plans for production themselves, will not allow it to be played within a sixty miles radius of London. Instead she was toying with the idea of Wedekind's *Lulu*, though only if playwright Peter Barnes would write a new version, one more appropriate to a woman of middle years than Wedekind's destructive slip of a girl.

Eventually, she decided to do Eugene O'Neill's infrequently performed *Strange Interlude*, which was due to open at The Duke of Yorks Theatre, in April 1984. It was another massive work, the playing time pared down to four and a half hours.

Then there is a film of a book by Russel Hoban with a screenplay by Harold Pinter and she hopes to follow that in the autumn of 1984 with Racine's *Phedre* as re-written by David Macdonald who wrote *Summit Conference*.

Conversations with Glenda

'You've talked of the kind of actor you despise. Whom do you admire?'

'Scofield. I haven't seen him for a long time, but to me he's the ideal of what acting should be about, a total absence of an intrusive self.'

'No mannerisms?'

'Well, a bit . . . . lately. But that's this country, isn't it? They don't know what to do with people. It's a disgrace that that kind of talent should not be harnessed somewhere. But where would we harness it here – the bloody National or the RSC?'

'You've been harnessed by the RSC.'

'I bloody haven't.'

'Well, you've been used by the RSC.'

'It was a two-way process. I stayed there as long as I found it useful and when I didn't, I left.'

'Like Scotfield did. And with the National as well.'

'He should go and work with Peter Brook again. I thought his Lear was wonderful. And Ralph Richardson is another one* He lives on a different time scale to the rest of us.'

'He's from another planet.'

'He's just extraordinary the *things* he's done!'

'So far you haven't mentioned any actresses.'

'Because there are so many – Vanessa, Maggie, Gemma Jones, Alison Steadman . . . . now I can't remember anybody else's name, but God, there are so many.

'That's what so irritating, there's such a richness of female talent and such a dearth of good female parts.'

'If there were more female dramatists there would be

---

* Ralph Richardson's death a week after this conversation took place does not, I believe, invalidate it.

more female roles. A male writer tends to see things from a male point of view.'

'Good female novelists don't slant their books with a female or feminist point of view. They reflect and are part of the society they inhabit. And this is not a society that sees women as major motivators or innovators.'

'Where are the women playwrights. There are a few but not many.'

'Nobody's helping them.'

'Who helps anyone to write plays?'

'Wives. Women have to function at a lot of other things as well. It's entirely okay for a man to drop his family, his friends or his social life for the call of his profession, but it's not okay for a woman.'

'That would be valid if there were no women writers. There are plenty. The shortage is of women playwrights.'

'Yes, but to write a novel is a very different process from writing a play.'

'Yes, it usually takes less time. There are certainly fewer words.'

'But where a play happens – in the theatre – it's very hard for a woman; it's made hard for them.'

★   ★   ★

'Are you actually doing this course on the Humanities at Thames Polytechnic?'

'No, I only made inquiries. They said I'd have to submit an essay and they'd have to plead a special case for me and because I didn't do it I thought that was the end of that. Then I got a letter from the guy at Thames – and I didn't leak it to the Press – and he asked if they were going to get my essay and I wrote back and said not now but I'll have another go next year. Perhaps.'

'All the things I've read said you were doing it.'

'You ought to know by now that you shouldn't believe what you read in the papers.'

'I think I'll write a foreword to this book which says that when I quote Glenda Jackson as having said something she's said it, and when I quote her as having said something to someone else I hope she's said it. Over and over again I have read that you are going to give up acting and take up social work or politics.'

'I'll tell you precisely what I mean. I'm not going to hang about for twenty-odd years waiting for someone to cast me in the old lady roles. I'm now at an age where there really aren't roles for a woman of my years so what am I going to do? I'm not going to sit at home and polish the furniture. So I'll do something else. But when the work stops being interesting I'll stop.'

'What's the longest you've ever had between projects since the *Marat/Sade*?'

'About six months. That was after my son was born. And that was choice.'

'And he's now 14. So if you didn't get a decent script you could take a few months off surely and relax a bit. Can you relax?'

'I'm not aware of being unrelaxed. But I am more a work person than a non-work person.'

'I meant just to take a little time off, to be patient until the right script comes along.'

'That's what's so bloody irritating. I've been working for about 27 years and I should now be being worked to my fullest capacity. I should really be being *worked* now. So should all actresses of my years – and not be in this endless one-off situation of doing a play and then wondering if there's something else you'll want to do. There should be a way of structuring the system so that you can actually exercise all that practice.'

'It seems to me that you're talking about joining a company –'

'What's the good of that; the parts aren't there.'

'– where you will discuss what roles you want to play for the next 12 or 18 months.'

'No major company is going to stage a female-oriented season. If you do a season at the RSC, you'd only get two parts, possibly. It's unlikely that they'd do a season which had all those cracking women's parts in it because there aren't that many, even in Shakespeare.'

* * *

'How many cigarettes a day do you smoke?'

'I've stopped counting. I'm not up to two packets yet. About 30.'

'You once said you had a lot of fears – fear of flying accidents, fear of being disabled, fear of first nights, fear even of just going onto the stage.'

'I have.'

'Why aren't you afraid of cigarettes?'

'They're so – distant. The others happen at the moment.'

* * *

'Did you ever say that an actress needs to be able to laugh and to cry and that when you need to laugh you think of your sex life and when you need to cry you think of your sex life?'

'No.'

* * *

'You've contradicted and demolished every theory on acting that I've cobbled together over 20 years of watching and writing about it.'

'That's all right; there are as many theories as there are actors.'

* * *

THINGS SHE HAS SAID: 'Why can't you say "yes" to sex and "no" to pregnancy? I'm extremely suspicious of people who, on the one hand, say we must protect the sanctity of life and at the same time say we must increase our defence budget. . . . How dare they condemn a child to be born to a mother who doesn't want it?' – Interview in *Time Out*, August 20, 1976.

'Grow you buggers, grow!' – following a television gardener's advice that people should talk to their plants.

'When I heard the BBC was putting on a retrospective season of my films I thought, "Oh my God, I must have died." '

★   ★   ★

THINGS SAID ABOUT HER: 'You cannot look at this woman without feeling you've matured five years at least.' – Peter Hall, Director of the National Theatre.

'In a sense to work with her is the same as to meet her. She's direct, uncomplicated, honest, very alive. She's absolutely without machination or ulterior motives. She can be fun. She often is. But of all the actors I've worked with she has a capacity for work that's phenomenal. There's immense power of concentration, a great deal of attack, thrust, determination. She searches hard. It's quite ruthless.' – Trevor Nunn, Director of the Royal Shakespeare Theatre.

It has not been possible to discuss in detail all the films and plays in which Glenda Jackson has appeared. Some, especially the films, are hardly worth discussing except to speculate on why she agreed to make them. Two things, though, are certain: it would not have been for the money and there would have been something in the character or in the words that excited her, that made her feel that here was a role that would repay exploration. It could well be that she has, in some cases, had to persuade herself of this for the alternative would have been to wait until something with more obvious merit came along. That would mean being idle. You don't have to believe in God to know for sure that the devil makes work for idle hands.

The truth is that her judgement, like her acting, is acute, intelligent and instinctual, but the work ethic is in the driving seat and his name is Jehu.

Glenda Jackson's Films:

1967: *The Marat/Sade*, directed by Peter Brook
1968: *Negatives*, directed by Peter Medak
1968 *Tell Me Lies*, directed by Peter Brook,
1969: *Women in Love*, directed by Ken Russell,
1970: *The Music Lovers*, directed by Ken Russell
1971: *Sunday Bloody Sunday*, directed by John Schlesinger,
1971: *Mary Queen of Scots*, directed by Charles Jarrott
1972: *Triple Echo*, directed by Michael Apted
1972: *A Touch of Class*, directed by Melvin Frank
1973: *Bequest to the Nation*, directed by James Cellan Jones
1973: *The Tempter*, directed by Damiano Damiani
1974: *The Romantic Englishwoman*, directed by Joseph Losey
1974: *The Maids*, directed by Christopher Miles
1975: *Hedda Gabler*, directed by Trevor Nunn
1975: *The Incredible Sarah*, directed by Richard Fleischer
1976: *Nasty Habits*, directed by Michael Lindsay Hogg
1977: *House Calls*, directed by Howard Zieff
1977: *The Class of Miss McMichael*, directed by Silvio Narrizano
1978: *Stevie*, directed by Robert Enders
1979: *Hopscotch*, directed by Richard Neame
1979: *Health*, directed by Robert Altman
1981: *The Patricia Neal Story*, directed by Anthony Page and Anthony Harvey
1981: *The Return of the Soldier*, directed by Alan Bridges
1982: *Giro City*, directed by Karl Francis

Glenda Jackson's Plays

1957 – 1962:   Worthing, Hornchurch, Crewe repertory companies, various minor tours.

1962:   Alexandra in *The Idiot*, Lyric, Hammersmith.

1963:   Siddie in *Alfie*, Mermaid/Duchess.

1964:   Theatre of Cruelty, LAMDA, Charlotte Corday in the *Marat/Sade*

1965:   The Princess of France in *Love's Labour's Lost*; Ophelia in *Hamlet*, Royal Shakespeare Company, Stratford-on-Avon. Eva in Brecht's *Puntila*, Aldwych

1965:   American debut in the *Marat/Sade*, Martin Beck Theatre, New York.

1966:   *US*, RSC, Aldwych

1967:   Masha in *Three Sisters*, Royal Court

1967:   Tamara Fanghorn in *Fanghorn*, Arts Theatre, London.

1973:   *The Collaborators*, Duchess Theatre

1974:   *The Maids*, Greenwich Theatre

1975:   *Hedda Gabler*, Aldwych

1976:   *The White Devil*, Old Vic

1977:   *Stevie*, Vaudeville Theatre

1978:   *Antony and Cleopatra*, Stratford-on-Avon / Aldwych

1980:   *Rose*, Albery Theatre

1982:   *Summit Conference*, Lyric Theatre

1983:   *Great and Small*, Vaudeville Theatre